Beading

with Right Angle

Weave

Beading
with Right Angle
Weave

Christine Prussing

A **BEADWORK**®
HOW-TO BOOK

INTERWEAVE PRESS
www.interweave.com

Editor: Christine Townsend
Technical Editor: Dustin Wedekind
Illustration: Marjorie C. Leggitt
Design: Karen Schober
Production: Samantha L. Thaler, Dean Howes
Photography: Joe Coca
Photo Styling: Ann Swanson
Proofreader and Indexer: Nancy Arndt

Interweave Press, Inc.
201 East Fourth Street
Loveland, CO 80537 USA
www. interweave. com

Printed in Singapore by Imago

Library of Congress Cataloging-in-Publication Data

Prussing, Christine, 1948-
  Beading with right angle weave : a beadwork how-to book / Christine Prussing.
      p. cm.
  Includes bibliographical references and index.
  ISBN 1-931499-50-0
  1. Beadwork. I. Title.
  TT860.P78 2004
  745.58'2--dc22
                              2004006409

10 9 8 7 6 5 4 3 2 1

Table *of* Contents

WALCO ... CRAFTS BOOKLET N°21

Wood Bead Craft

INSTRUCTIONS and DESIGNS
for the making of

BAGS · NECKLACES · BRACELETS · BELTS

Walco
37 WEST 37th ST.

Introduction and a Bit of History

Right-angle weave beading is easy to

do. It's a generous and forgiving method of

beadwork because it doesn't demand careful

scrutiny and endless bead culling; instead, you

can mix all sorts of bead sizes and shapes in

inventive ways. Results can be slinky and flexible,

or rigid enough to form small sculptures. It can

be lacy or geometric. Right-angle weave can

also require forethought, intense focus, and

precision—it's fun to explore new pathways

and get the brain cells sparking!

The phrase "right-angle weave" was coined by bead artist Virginia Blakelock sometime in the early 1980's. Inspecting a piece of African beadwork, she noticed that, unlike netted beadwork where the beads lie more or less in the same direction like stacks of plates, adjacent beads in this piece lay at right angles to each other. A closer look also revealed that threads actually crossed in opposite directions through certain beads, again unlike netting, where the threads tend to lie parallel to one another. Perspicaciously, Virginia decided to distinguish this type of beadwork mesh from netting by calling it "right-angle weave."

In her book *Those Bad, Bad Beads*, Virginia described and diagrammed a method for accomplishing this weave by using a single thread with a needle on each end and starting the beadwork in the middle of the thread. Later, David Chatt adopted and popularized Virginia's phrase to describe a right-angle beadwork mesh created by a clockwise-counterclockwise circling method using a single needle, similar to the way daisy chains are worked. So, we now have a single phrase describing two different working methods—one using two needles, the other only one.

Beadwork done with right-angle weave turns up in collections of beaded artifacts from around the world—Europe, Africa, Russia, Southeast Asia, and the Americas. As natural fiber threads are subject to rot, however, intact beadwork more than a few centuries old is often difficult to find. We do know of historical examples of right-angle weave from Britain and the United States that date from the seventeenth century

("1630 Remember the Pore" beaded bag illustrated in Crabtree and Stallebrass, *Beadwork: A World Guide*). We know, too, that beads were recycled. As Elena Moiseenko and Valerie Faleeva wryly note in their book *Beadwork and Bugle in Russia, 18th–Early 20th Century*, "Peasant women, inclined to thrift, do not keep [beaded decorations] but unravel them mercilessly and use the beads for new, present-day things."

Despite the scarcity of millennia-old specimens, I suspect that right-angle weave was used whenever there were plentiful beads to string, because it is an easily intuited method for creating a secure, flexible mesh of beads. Crossing the threads in opposite directions through a bead or beads serves a function similar to tying an overhand knot, and the technique is a natural progression for anyone familiar with netting, basketry, knotting, braiding, or lace making. Children make this weave when they construct little bead-woven animal charms from plastic line and "pony" beads. Bead artists who use wire instead of thread to make their designs also adopt right-angle weave as one of their working methods. The weave is a perennial in the fashion industry, often appearing as purses woven of beads made from wood or plastic. Needlework and craft pamphlets demonstrating this type of bead stringing can be found dating from the nineteenth century to the present. The *Walco Bead-Crafts Booklet No. 21: Wood Bead Craft, 1937* is a treasure trove of right-angle weave patterns for accessories. In her *Pearl and Bead Boutique Book*, Virginia Nathanson devotes an entire chapter to stringing chokers, necklaces, belts, and bracelets using right-angle weave and faux pearls. In the jewelry trade, coral necklaces and bracelets from Italy, garnet jewelry from India, and pearl jewelry from China use right-angle weave to string the beads. And then there's that ubiquitous item, the car seat mat of large, wooden beads woven together with monofilament. In short, right-angle weave is everywhere!

This book provides what I hope are enjoyable projects for developing basic skills with right-angle weave, but I'd like to think that it will also enable you to take off in new directions and design amazing things all on your own.

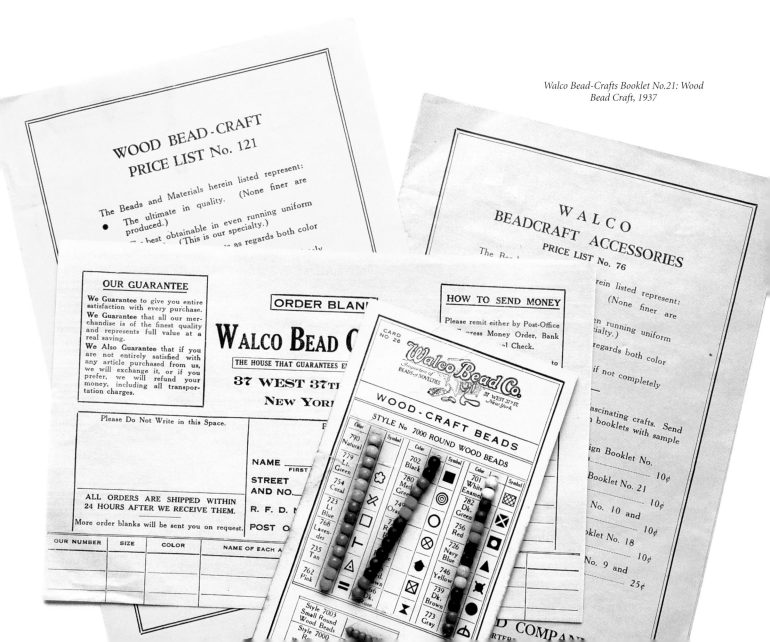

Walco Bead-Crafts Booklet No.21: Wood Bead Craft, 1937

Chapter One

Materials and Tools

Having the right tools on hand for

any job may not guarantee your success,

but it sure helps. Here, you'll find every-

thing you need to get going, including

beads, stringing materials, needles,

and hand tools.

BEADS

One of the nice features of right-angle weave is that it's not fussy about the beads having to be all the same size. It's easy to attain an even-looking fabric of seed beads without relentlessly culling the beads to ensure they're all identical in size. In fact, many attractive right-angle woven designs depend upon using different-sized beads.

The exception to the above rule is when you're using bugle or cylinder beads (Figure 1), because they tend to accentuate the par-

Figure 1. Cylinder or bugle beads

allel lines of the resulting bead mesh, our eyes immediately pick up any unevenness. However, rather than using a micrometer on each bead to assure identical size, stringing a rounded bead at each angle between the longer beads will work wonders to even out

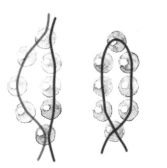

Figure 2. Netting versus right-angle weave

the appearance of the bead fabric. Those who have a large stock of Japanese cylinder beads might especially take note of this effect and try combinations of cylinder beads with Czech seed beads.

Another advantage of right-angle weave when you're working with spherical beads such as pearls or gemstones is that, unlike netting (Figure 2), it causes the beads to lie evenly rather than jostle for position to achieve the shortest thread path.

STRINGING MATERIALS

Right-angle weave reduces strain on the thread and produces a noticeably more flexible, supple bead fabric. Folded or bent, a right-angle weave is far less likely to snap threads or break beads. This flexibility, however, comes at the price of more visible thread. Because the bead holes cannot butt up against one another, the connecting thread inevitably shows between the beads. However, rather than detracting from the beadwork, in right-angle weave the more visible thread can be used to advantage to achieve interesting textural or color-blend effects.

How much of your stringing materials should you use? Instructors will invariably suggest, with good reason, that students use about a yard of thread at a time. Longer threads tend to tangle and twist and time is wasted thread-wrangling rather than beading. That said, I have yet to meet a beader who doesn't use at least an outstretched-arm's length of thread, or anywhere from five to ten feet. Long threads seem easier to use than threading more needles and tying more knots. Use whatever thread length you can stand, and simply start with longer thread tails that you shorten as the work progresses.

NYLON Probably the most popular beading threads in the United States are nylons, straight filaments such as in Nymo, C-lon, rod winding, and twisted (plied, spun) filaments as in Silamide and Conso cord. Since these threads are used industrially on a large scale, they are usually treated: 1) with a mild glue so they'll stay wound on small machine bobbins, 2) with silicone or other waxes to provide lubrication and reduce fuzzing and lint in sewing machines, 3) with heat-setting to reduce fuzzing and stretch. The standard advice for persuading nylon threads to go through the eye of a beading needle is to cut the thread end at an angle—once the filaments at the point are through the needle, the others can line up and follow. Threads with a twist, such as Silamide, can have a few filaments teased out at the end and twisted with a bit of wax or thread conditioner to make a finer thread tip that will then draw the remainder of the thread through the needle's eye. Pinching a nylon thread end closely between the tips of one's index finger and thumb also helps align the filaments in close order so that the needle's eye can be lowered onto them. Beeswax or thread conditioner can be used to tame unwanted curling in nylon. A drop of jeweler's glue will seal knots to prevent them from untying. Nylon threads possess the additional charm of being inexpensive and widely available in many beautiful colors.

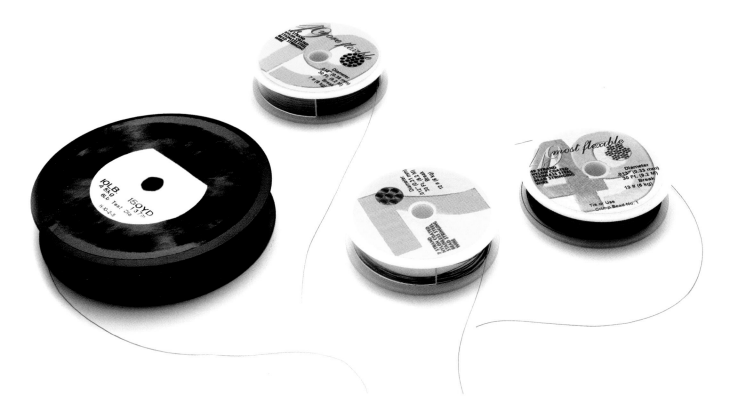

POWERPRO I quit using nylon threads the minute I discovered PowerPro—a waxed, braided polyethylene line. Because it is a round four-ply braid, PowerPro tends to stay put once threaded onto a needle, and it doesn't require any further attention during two-needle work. Other attractions include great strength and abrasion resistance, flexibility without annoying slipperiness, almost no stretch, imperviousness to water, and resistance to common chemicals such as bleach. Knots are easy to tie and they stay put without glue; strangely, they're also easy to tease apart with a needle, if necessary, without damage to the line. Since the braid doesn't stretch or fuzz, it's possible to reuse it. So if you have to tear out your beadwork, at least you can recycle your thread—a good thing, because PowerPro thread is expensive. It will not accept dye, so the only colors available are those of the waxes used to make the extremely slippery polyethylene fibers manageable—a neutral mossy green, white, or high-visibility yellows and pinks (the line is also a favorite amongst fishermen). This wax can powder off a bit when a new length of line is run through a needle, but it's non-toxic and easily blown away with a puff of breath. It does not subsequently flake off onto the beadwork. I like the 10-pound test size best for most right-angle weave, although the 20-pound test can be useful with large or heavy beads. The 8-pound test is delightfully supple and silky, but like the nylons, it can slip out of the needle eye at inopportune moments. Very sharp scissors are required to cut this line; children's Fiskars

are perfect because they're sharp and the blades are angled for a clean cut.

To thread PowerPro, first flatten the round braid by pulling the thread end between your fingernails or a jeweler's pliers. Align the flattened thread end with the needle eye, and pinch the eye of the threaded needle lightly but firmly between your thumb and forefinger, keeping the thread at a right angle to the needle and centered in the eye as you pull it through. Avoid jamming the thread into a corner of the eye, or you run the risk of destroying the needle. Unlike nylon, if a PowerPro thread end becomes unbraided, it's actually easier to thread through a needle. The fine individual filaments can easily be made to cling together simply by dipping the thread end into water and pulling the thread through your fingers to straighten it—no wax or conditioner required.

FIRELINE is another polyethylene braid, the fibers coated with an additional layer of plastic after the line is braided. It tends to be flatter and more easily threaded than PowerPro, albeit a bit stiffer. The colorant used to tint the surface a neutral gray can come off on your hands, but it's non-toxic (again, it is a popular fishing line). I like PowerPro so much that I am not even tempted to work with anything else, but I do hear good reports from other beaders about Fireline in the 6-pound test size.

MONOFILAMENT fishing lines, although widely scorned for use in beadwork, are actually quite popular for fashion jewelry and accessories. Japanese beaders use these lines with great success in their right-angle weave designs. Monofilaments generally don't require the use of a needle, which can be a definite plus for doing beadwork with children. A surgeon's knot (See Knots and Starting New Thread, page 18) holds reasonably well in monofilament. A small jeweler's pliers and a drop of glue will work wonders in persuading monofilament knots to stay tied. Line sizes useful in right-angle weave range from 6- to 15-pound test.

BEADING WIRE is a twisted steel cable encased in a nylon coating. The cable varies among a twist of three, seven, nineteen, or forty-nine strands. The higher number of strands per cable, the more flexible it is, but also the more expensive. Size of the wires in the cable determines the finished diameter, from .012 to .024 inch. Thin wires are more difficult to cable without snapping, so a high number of strands in a smaller diameter cable also results in a high price. The cable coatings can be colored, or the cables themselves can be plated to appear golden. While the standard gray cables can be unattractive for use with transparent beads, the colored and plated varieties have opened up new possibilities in bead design, especially for gemstone beads and cut-lead crystal, such as Swarovski products. Crimp beads are used to secure cable ends, and are available in a variety of sizes, shapes, and finishes. Special crimping pliers can be used with tubular crimp beads to minimize the appearance of the crimps. Those reluctant to do beadwork

with needle and thread will frequently plunge right in and use beading wire without hesitation—beading instructors take note!

LEATHER lacing in diameters of .5 to 1 mm works well with large-hole beads. Unlike cords such as satin rattail, the ends of leather cords don't fray, and leather is stiff enough to manipulate easily for stringing beads. Right-angle weave and large-hole beads are a match made in heaven for beaders whose manual dexterity is a problem, because the weave can produce more entertaining designs than simple stringing. If leather is outside your budget, a good substitute is braided polyester cord with the cut ends heated to fuse the fibers so they don't fan out during bead stringing.

NEEDLES

I have found standard 2" beading needles in size 10 or 12 to be most convenient for doing right-angle weave, because a long needle length is often required to accommodate large beads or stacks of beads. For situations involving small bead holes or multiple thread passes, thinner size 13 or 15 needles are handy to have on hand. Using a magnifier while threading needles will improve your manual dexterity.

When it comes to ripping out beadwork to correct a mistake, beaders are often tempted to backstitch through the fabric rather than remove the needle and pull the thread out. Alas, this is the road to ruin with right-angle weave, as backstitching will frequently result in accidental overhand knots being tied, not to mention thread-snagging by the needle. Bite the bullet and either pull your needle back eye-first through the beadwork, or take the needle(s) off the thread(s).

Once the needles are removed, beads woven with double-needle right-angle weave are easily pulled off the thread ends; however, single-needle weave must be teased apart with a sewing needle or safety pin to loosen the weave and pull it out. Don't use your beading needle for this purpose unless you enjoy the challenge of working with bent needles. I keep a sewing needle handy with a length of thread tied onto the eye so I can easily find it on my beading tray or pull it from my needle case. A large safety pin is also a sturdy tool for teasing and pulling threads.

OTHER TOOLS AND SUPPLIES

BEAD DESIGN BOARD

BEAD SCOOP A bead scoop is essential for rounding up piles of beads and pouring them back into their containers. Jewelers use a variety of sizes and shapes for sorting gemstones and pearls, so you can simply pick whichever style suits you.

BEADING TRAY A small, flat tray or plate with a raised lip to prevent beads from escaping is sufficient. Line the tray with a fabric such as Ultrasuede, Vellux, corduroy, or velveteen. The fabric prevents the beads from sliding and rolling around, and makes them easy to pick up with a needle. Avoid fabrics with a weave, looped pile, or felted surface, because your needle will inevitably catch on the fibers and then spring loose

and send beads flying. For years I've used an 18 × 13" (46 × 32 cm) wooden tray that arrived one Christmas filled with dried fruit. I ate the fruit, cleaned up the tray, attached a square of Ultrasuede with masking tape, and the tray has worked beautifully ever since. I often bead sitting in an armchair rather than at a table, with a pillow or blanket under the tray to stabilize it in my lap and raise it to a comfortable working height.

CUTTERS A pair of children's Fiskar scissors, small in size and with rounded tips, is my cutting tool of choice for PowerPro and other fabric threads.

An inexpensive pair of wire-cutters is also useful for dealing with beading wire, leather lacing, and monofilament.

A hot-point thread burner is a must-have item. About the size of a fat penlight, it has a fine wire loop tip that melts threads in a millisecond with the press of a button. Little thread ends can be annoyingly visible and impossible to reach with the scissors, but they're easily melted into invisibility with the thread burner. Using a magnifier while thread burning is recommended—you certainly don't want to accidentally melt surrounding threads in your beadwork. This tool has become my favorite item for clipping the thread ends from knots.

GLUE Hypo-Tube cement manufactured by Germanow-Simon is my favorite for beadwork, because the tube has a needlepoint applicator that can fit inside a bead hole. Use with good ventilation and avoid getting it on your skin, as it contains xylene and heptane. Do not use Hypo-Tube for projects with children.

LIGHTING Halogen task lamps or reading lamps give the best color definition; just keep away from the hot little bulb. Small, folding fluorescent lamps with a daylight-equivalent tube also work well; look for the 13-watt size.

MAGNIFIER Many types of magnifiers are available that are either worn like a hat, attached to a glasses frame, free-standing on a table, or attached to a task lamp. My favorite is the Optivisor, beloved for decades by jewelers, watchmakers, lapidaries, medical and dental professionals, and machinists. Its sturdy, comfortable, no-nonsense industrial design makes the Optivisor lightweight and portable, impossible to wear out, easy to fling onto your head at a moment's notice without removing your glasses, and guaranteed to ruin your hairdo. Its glass lenses are scratch-resistant (unlike cheaper acrylic lenses), and can be switched out or replaced. An optional loupe attachment provides even closer magnification. The higher the magnification, the closer you must hold the work to your eyes.

MASKING TAPE is essential for tacking beadwork in place while you're using two needles. A safety pin, straight pin, or beading needle can also come in handy for this purpose. Fly fishermen use a third-hand tool when they're winding flies; you might want to borrow one and give it a test drive for beadwork.

PLIERS Purchase as fine-tipped a pair of chain-nose pliers as you can afford. This tool is invaluable for untying knots, gently pulling reluctant needles through beads, tugging on thin, slippery thread ends to tighten knots, straightening bent needles, and picking up tiny beads.

A fine-tipped pair of round-nose pliers is also useful.

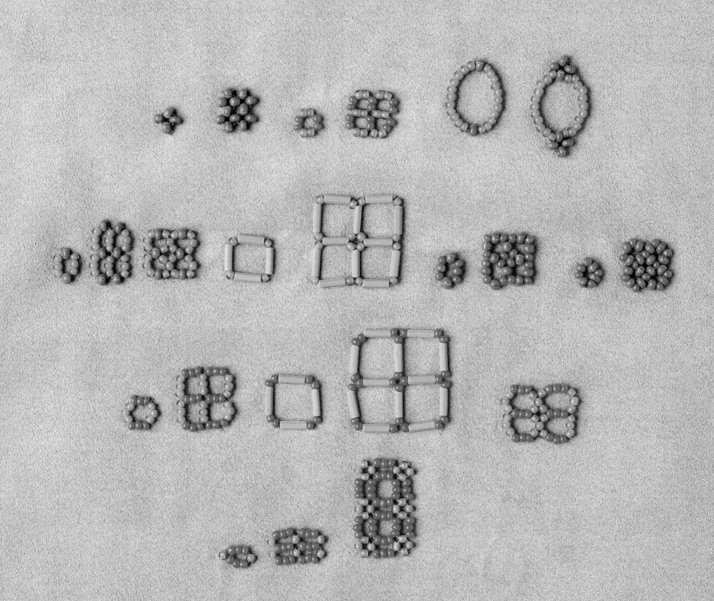

Chapter Two

Basics

Beading with right-angle weave

isn't hard to learn or master if you know

its basic building blocks. In this chapter,

you'll start out with simple, easy-to-manip-

ulate bead configurations, and move into

real right-angle weave projects that make

you look (and feel!) like a pro.

READ THIS FIRST

The simplest unit, from which right-angle weave derives its name, is comprised of four beads arranged like the leaves of a four-leaf clover. That is, each bead lies at a right angle to its two immediate neighbors. In this book, we'll refer to these four bead positions as the cardinal points on a compass—North, South, East, and West. Note the word "positions." We'll also use the term "unit" rather than "stitch" as shorthand for the individual working units (Figure 1). As mentioned in

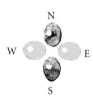

Figure 1. 1 × 1 unit compass diagram

the introduction, a right-angle weave can be accomplished by two different working methods, with corresponding different sequences of bead stringing and pass throughs. Nonetheless, at the end of a unit the basic North-South-East-West 90°-angle positioning of the beads is always the same.

In later chapters I will simply list which beads fill each of the N-S-E-W positions, thereby allowing you to choose whichever thread path you need to connect the beads together. It won't matter if you're working with two threads, or working a single thread either clockwise or counterclockwise, the final bead arrangement will be the same.

Just as explorers use a compass or GPS to navigate the trackless wastes, you'll find my little mental N-S-E-W compass of great help when navigating any right-angle weave pattern you encounter, enabling you to confidently deal with turns, diagonals, complex color combinations, and three-dimensional work. Keep in mind that each time you turn the work, these directionals remain the same; for example: if you start working on a North-South unit, and you turn it clockwise, the West side now becomes North.

A row is a length composed of consecutive individual units. Although right-angle weave can be worked in any direction, for the projects in this book the beadwork rows will proceed vertically, from South to North, each row growing like bamboo from bottom to top. Rows will be added next to one another like books on a shelf. When you're using two needles, it makes no difference to which side of the beadwork additional rows are added; however, when you're using a single needle to work a row along the left side of the beadwork, a right-handed person may find such a work progression awkward—likewise for a left-handed person working along the right side. Holding the work below where the weaving is taking place (rather than alongside) often resolves this difficulty, as does placing the beadwork on a working surface instead of holding it in one hand.

The number of units per row is counted by the beads that stick out so conveniently, like elbows, from the edges of the beadwork.

Figure 2. 3 × 5 rows

These are the beads lying horizontally along the East/West axis. When you're counting units along an edge of beadwork, rotate the edge so that it runs vertically, from South to North, and there will then be no mistaking which beads are the ones lying East/West for the tallying of the number of units.

MULTIBEAD UNITS

As we'll discover in Chapter 5, Chains, many interesting right-angle weaves depart from the basic four-bead unit and substitute multiple-bead stacks in any or all of the East/West and North/South positions. Rather than resembling a cloverleaf/diamond/cross, these units more closely resemble variations on a square or rectangle. Whenever we refer to a rectangular object in daily life we describe it in terms of length and width. For example, a certain piece of lumber is described as a "two-by-four" (2×4) instead of "$2 \times 4 \times 2 \times 4$" or "twelve around." Likewise these multibead right-angle weave units can be described in terms of bead numbers per length and width; for example, "2×4" means two beads down in each of the East and West positions, and four beads across in the South and North positions.

When you're working adjacent rows in the 3×1 or 3×3 units, a different effect results from joining all the beads in a three-bead stack, as opposed to using only the middle bead in the stack as a connection point. Or consider the three-row matrix in the last row of the photo on page 12: 1) the first row alternates 1×1 "short" and 3×1 "long" units; 2) the second row alternates 1×3 "flat" with 3×3 "fat" units; 3) the third row again alternates 1×1 and 3×1 short and long units.

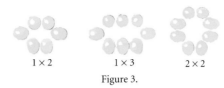

1×2 1×3 2×2

Figure 3.

PASS THROUGH VS PASS BACK THROUGH

"Pass through" means running the thread through a bead again, in the same direction as the first stringing or the progression of the weave. When working a four-bead picot or a figure-eight, you'll use a pass through.

"Pass back through" means running the thread through a bead again in the reverse direction to the original stringing. A pass back through can result in threads lying parallel in the bead hole, as in netting, or the threads crossing, as in double-needle right-angle weave.

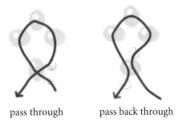

pass through   pass back through

READING PATTERNS

Regardless whether a pattern is worked with a single needle or two needles, the final bead from which the thread(s) emerge(s) at the end of a unit is indicated by a circle with an *x* inside, and will be referred to as the *crossing* bead. The circled *x* will alternate from red to black to assist you in following the patterns from one unit to the next. The

NOTES

Consider each unit on its own and pay attention to the North-South-East-West positions of the beads, not the thread path.

When you're following a diagram, or planning the next unit, note the bead(s) from which your thread(s) emerge(s) at the beginning of a unit. This is your South/starting position for the unit.

Next decide which beads are going to be in the East, North, and West positions.

Observe from which bead(s) the thread will emerge at the end of the unit in order to decide whether you will be working a straight line and emerging through North, or whether you will be making a 90° turn to one side and emerging on the East or West.

You'll notice, when you carefully consider the following examples:

- *Each unit involves stringing three beads.*

- *When you're making a 90° turn using two needles, all three beads are strung on one needle, and the other needle simply crosses through the last bead.*

- *When you're making a 90° turn using one needle, it makes a difference whether the unit must proceed clockwise or counterclockwise; sometimes only one of the three new beads must be passed through again, sometimes all three have to be passed through.*

circle indicating the end of one unit is the *South* or *starting* bead for the next unit. Our sample diagram shows four units: three vertical, and the fourth a 90° turn to the East.

Four units

NEEDLE METHODS

There are three different methods for accomplishing the four-unit in the sample diagram (above). Referring to the color-coded diagrams, here's how the three methods might be worked.

TWO NEEDLES

STEP 1: String 1 pink bead and position it in the center of the thread. String 1 yellow on the right, 1 orange on the left. Use one needle to string 1 green bead and pass the other needle back through the green bead.

STEP 2: String 1 purple on the right, 1 blue on the left. Use one needle to string 1 pink bead and pass the other needle back through the pink bead.

STEP 3: Repeat Step 1, without stringing a pink bead.

STEP 4: String 1 blue, 1 pink, and 1 purple on the left. Pass the right needle back through the purple bead.

Two needles

STEP 4: Make a counterclockwise turn to East. String 1 purple, 1 pink, and 1 blue bead, pass through the green bead from left to right, then up again through the purple bead.

Single-needle, clockwise start

SINGLE NEEDLE, CLOCKWISE START

STEP 1: String 1 green, 1 yellow, 1 pink, and 1 orange bead. Pass through the green bead again to form a 4-bead diamond. Arrange it with the orange bead to the West, the yellow to the East, and the green bead to the North.

STEP 2: Make a counterclockwise circle. String 1 purple, 1 pink, and 1 blue bead. Pass through the green bead from left to right, then up again through the purple and pink beads.

STEP 3: Make a clockwise circle. String 1 orange, 1 green, and 1 yellow bead. Pass through the pink bead from right to left, then up again through the orange and green beads.

SINGLE NEEDLE, COUNTERCLOCKWISE START

STEP 1: String 1 green, 1 orange, 1 yellow, and 1 green bead, and pass through the green bead again to form a 4-bead diamond. Arrange it as for Step 1 above.

STEP 2: Make a clockwise circle. String 1 blue, 1 pink, and 1 purple, pass through the green bead from right to left, then up again through the blue and pink beads.

STEP 3: Make a counterclockwise circle. String 1 yellow, 1 green, and 1 orange bead, pass through the pink bead from left to right, then up again through the yellow and green beads.

STEP 4: Make a clockwise turn to East. String 1 blue, 1 pink, and 1 purple bead, pass

NOTES

When you're using two needles to add one row alongside another, first do the pass through of the bead on the adjacent row, and then string the new beads on the other needle. Working this way makes it easier to decipher stripes and color changes. The South starting bead and the pass-through bead are known quantities, so get them out of the way first; then, you only have to deal with two beads.

Avoid snagging thread. Snags make the weave difficult to tighten, and will cause aggravation should a unit have to be unraveled. When you're passing a needle through a bead and want to avoid snagging the threads in the middle, imagine you're trying to scrape the wall of the bead with the needle. If you feel the needle tip entering thread, pull it back out and try again.

When you do snag a thread, immediately put the work down and take a deep breath. Remember that you're a right-angle samurai, and must maintain a Zen attitude of cool detachment. Have a sip of tea and help yourself to a bon-bon. Once calm has been restored, pull the needle(s) off the thread and gently pull the snag free. After a few such episodes, you'll develop a feel for when the needle tip has penetrated thread, and know when to immediately stop and back it out. You'll also have become very good at rethreading needles.

When you're unraveling a unit, take the needle(s) off the thread end(s). Don't try to backstitch through the unit—the odds are high that you'll tie over-hand knots and snag thread. If you're feeling lucky and just need to get the needle back through a bead or two, loosen up enough thread so that you can pull the needle backward eye-first through the weave, bead by bead.

through the green bead from right to left, then again through the blue, pink, and purple beads.

Single-needle, counterclockwise start

KNOTS AND STARTING NEW THREAD

For beadwork that covers something else and doesn't flex or move around much, knots aren't really necessary. Right-angle weave doesn't tend to ravel. Just start the new thread a few units back from the last unit of the old thread. If you like, apply a bit of jeweler's glue to the thread ends and weave them back through a few units. Trim the ends when the glue is dry, about 20 minutes later.

For beadwork that is likely to be flexed frequently, such as jewelry, the square knot and its close cousin the surgeon's knot serve well to keep the thread ends from working themselves loose. They both have the benefit of being what sailors call "collapsible" knots—in other words, pulling on one end will loosen the knot and make it slip. This feature enables the knot to be positioned and concealed inside a bead by alternately tugging one end or the other and then retightening the knot by pulling both ends.

To tie a square knot, leave the needle on the thread that's emerging from the bead inside which you've decided to conceal the knot. If there's a needle on the other thread end, take it off. Tie the knot thus: needle thread over no-needle thread, tighten; then needle thread back over no-needle thread again. Pass the needle back through the bead, and pull the thread ends to position and tighten the knot inside this bead.

Square knot

A surgeon's knot has one extra overhand pass: needle thread over no-needle thread, tighten; then needle thread back over no-needle thread and back over no-needle thread. A surgeon's knot is more secure than a square knot, but bulkier, so some bead holes may not allow it.

Tighten knots slowly and carefully so you'll have fewer problems with thread twists and snarls.

Tie as many knots as will make you feel secure that your work won't come apart. I usually tie two, separated by one unit.

When starting a new thread for single-needle right-angle weave, tie a square knot close to the work, using the thread ends, leaving 6" tails, and continue weaving. When you are ready to trim the thread ends, position the knot inside a bead to conceal it, then weave the tails around through a few adjacent units before trimming them. As mentioned above, a bit of jeweler's glue smoothed onto the tails before weaving them in will help keep them in place when the glue is dried.

Starting in a new thread for two-needle right-angle weave is very easy (two-needle thread splice). Tie a square knot as above and conceal it inside an East or West bead (to minimize the amount of thread passing through a bead). Starting two or three units back, center the new thread on a North or South bead, work each end through the last few units, and carry on. If any difficulty arises passing the needle and new thread through the bead with the knot inside it, pull one of the knot tails to drag the knot back out from inside the bead, pass the new thread through, and then reposition and tighten the knot inside the bead.

Starting thread

Chapter Three

Using Two Needles

Diagrams showing two-needle

beadwork are common. What these

diagrams cannot show, however, is

how the two needles are actually

manipulated.

Left to their own imaginations, beaders envision the beading process as being scary and difficult, equivalent to having to relearn how to write or sew or use chopsticks with the non-dominant hand. Even worse, they imagine that each needle must be worked separately, resulting in tangled threads and complicated, crisscrossing double thread paths. The image comes to mind of an unfortunate beader lying on the carpet, wrapped in her threads like a caterpillar in a cocoon.

In actual fact, if you can tie an overhand knot, you already possess the crucial manual dexterity necessary for two-needle beadwork. Isn't that a relief?

You don't believe me? Okay, let's develop the process slowly, working our way through the following fun exercise and simple projects.

EXERCISE WITH A SHOELACE

STEP 1: Find a shoelace, or a yard of round leather lacing or polyester cord, and some beads with large holes—plastic crow beads, for example.

STEP 2: String one bead, then fold the cord in half so that both ends are together and the bead is in the middle.

STEP 3: Holding one cord end in each hand, tie an overhand knot—right over left—and pull the cord ends to tighten the knot against the center bead.

STEP 4: Tie another overhand knot—left over right this time—and again pull the cord ends to tighten it. (Yes, that's correct; you've just tied a square knot.)

STEP 5: Notice that in tying and tightening these knots, your fingers automatically switch the cord ends they're holding: after each knot, what started out as the left-hand cord end is now in your right hand, and the right-cord end has migrated to your left hand.

STEP 6: Now, instead of tying an overhand knot, string a bead onto the end of the left-hand cord, and poke the right-hand cord end through the bead, coming from the opposite side. Pull the ends to tighten. As with tying knots, the cord ends have automatically switched from one hand to the other.

STEP 7: Try this again, this time stringing the bead onto the end of the right-hand cord, and crossing the left cord end through the bead.

STEP 8: Now string one bead onto each cord end and let these beads slide down the cord, where we can ignore them. Then, as before, string a bead onto one cord end, cross the other cord end through this bead, and pull the ends to tighten. Voilá! You've just done a right-angle weave unit.

STEP 9: Just for drill, repeat this last unit a few more times: String a bead on the right, a bead on the left, string a crossing bead, cross, tighten. Sometimes string the "crossing bead" on the right cord end, sometimes on the left.

Scoutmaster's Delight

Making the Scoutmaster's Delight is good practice for following a pattern, making right-angle turns, and learning your compass directions. The result is a lightweight lanyard that's easy for Mom to find in her backpack.

MATERIALS

- 1½ yd .5 mm leather or polyester cord
- 48 plastic 9 × 5mm crow beads Color A
- 11 plastic 9 × 6mm crow beads Color B
- Steel keychain split ring

The numbers in the illustration indicate the final crossing bead of each unit. That is, the bead from which the threads exit on each side when each unit is completed.

STEP 1: Follow Figure 1 for the 20 units that form the cross-shaped lanyard.

Unit 1: String 1 Color A (black) and the steel split ring. Fold your cord in half so that both ends are together and the bead and ring are in the middle of the thread. String 1 Color A on each thread, and then let these beads slide down the thread and ignore them. String 1 Color A on one thread and pass the other thread back through this bead.

Units 2 and 3: String 1 Color A on each thread, and then let these beads slide down the thread and ignore them. String 1 Color A on one thread and pass the other thread back through this bead.

Unit 4, a 90° turn to the East: String 3 Color B (red) on the left thread. Allow the first two beads to slide down the thread and hold the last bead near the thread end. Pass the right thread back through this bead and tighten. Rotate your work so that this last bead is now in the South position.

Units 5 and 6: Same as Unit 2.

Unit 7, a 90° turn to the West: String 3 Color B on the right thread, pass the left thread back through the last bead strung, and tighten. Rotate your work so that this last bead is now in the South position.

Unit 8: Same as Unit 2.

Unit 9, a 90° turn to the West: Same as Unit 7.

Unit 10: Same as Unit 2.

Unit 11, a 90° turn to the East: Same as Unit 4.

Unit 12: Same as Unit 2.

Unit 13, a 90° turn to the West: Same as Unit 7.

Unit 14: Same as Unit 2.

Unit 15, a 90° turn to the West: Same as Unit 7.

Unit 16: Same as Unit 2.

Unit 17, a 90° turn to the East: Same as Unit 4.

Unit 18: Same as Unit 2.

Unit 19, a 90° turn to the West: Same as Unit 7.

Unit 20: Same as Unit 2.

Unit 21, a 90° turn to the West: Same as Unit 7.

Unit 22: Same as Unit 2.

Unit 23, a 90° turn to the West: String 1 Color A on the right thread, pass through the Color B bead indicated (part of Unit 4) from right to left, and string 1 Color A. Pass the left thread back through this last bead, tighten, then rotate the work so that this bead is in the South position.

STEP 2: Form the center circle of beads. Pass the right thread through 1 Color B and 1 Color A immediately to the East, then string 3 Color A, pass to the West through the opposite Color B indicated in the illustration, then string 1 Color B.

Use the left thread to string 3 Color A, pass through the opposite Color B, then pass back through the last bead strung to the East.

STEP 3: Holding both thread tails parallel and together, tie an overhand knot and tighten it as close as you can to the last bead added. String 1 Color A on one thread tail and tie an overhand knot near the end to keep the bead from slipping off. Repeat with 1 Color B on the other thread tail.

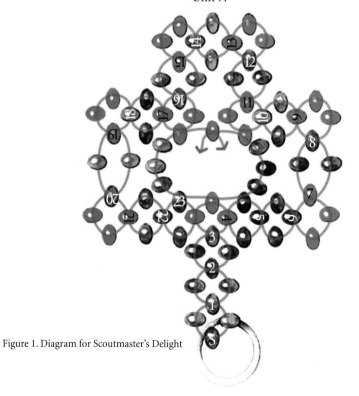

Figure 1. Diagram for Scoutmaster's Delight

Rainbow Lanyard

For this stylin' zipper pull, use smaller beads and monofilament: practice adding rows to the starting chain and making a tube. You'll also use the square knot and surgeon's knot.

MATERIALS

- *Size 6° seed beads, 12 beads each in red, orange, yellow, green, turquoise, blue, purple, and pink*
- *1 yd 10lb test monofilament*
- *1' of 1–5 mm leather lacing*
- *10mm split ring*
- *25mm split ring or a lanyard hook*
- *9 × 6mm crow bead*
- *Masking tape*

STEP 1: See Figure 1. String 1 orange bead on the monofilament line. Fold the line in half so that both ends are together and the orange bead is in the middle.

Row 1, Units 1–10: String 1 red on the left line, 1 yellow on the right. On either line, string 1 orange and pass the other line back through this bead. Pull to tighten. If necessary, reposition the resulting 4-bead diamond so that it is in the center of the line, then use masking tape to hold it to your work surface. Loosen and refasten the tape as needed while you work through the pattern.

Unit 11: Make a right-angle turn to the East. String 1 red, 1 orange, and 1 yellow on the left line, then pass the right thread back through the yellow bead. Unfasten

Row 2

S

Row 1   Row 3

Figure 1. Diagram for Rainbow Lanyard

the masking tape and rotate your work so that the yellow bead is in the South position.

Row 2, Unit 1: Make a right-angle turn to the East. String 1 green, 1 turquoise, and 1 green on the left line, then pass the right line back through the last green bead strung. Rotate your work so that this bead is in the South position. Tape the work down again.

Units 2–10: Pass the right line upward through the adjacent yellow bead. String 1 turquoise and 1 green on the left line, then pass the right line back through the green bead.

Unit 11: Make a right-angle turn to the West. Pass the right line up through the adjacent last yellow bead, and then string 1 green and 1 turquoise bead. Pass the left line back through the turquoise bead. Rotate your work so that the turquoise bead is in the South position prior to the next unit.

Row 3, Unit 1: Make a right-angle turn to the West. String 1 blue, 1 purple, and 1 blue bead on the right line. Pass the left line back through the last blue bead strung. Rotate your work so that this blue bead is in the South position prior to the next unit.

Units 2–10: Pass the left line upward through the adjacent turquoise bead (use your right hand to help—just don't put the right line down, keep it tucked out of the way between your fingers). String 1 purple and 1 blue bead on the right line, then pass the left line back through the blue bead.

Unit 11: Make a right-angle turn to the East. Pass the left line through the adjacent last turquoise bead, and then string 1 blue and 1 purple bead. Pass the right line back through the purple bead. Rotate your work 180° so that this purple bead is in the West position.

STEP 2:   In the fourth row we'll roll the beadwork into a tube around the leather lacing, attach the small split ring to the larger one, thread the lacing through the smaller split ring, and then fold the lacing in half and lay it on top of your beadwork, taping down the ends (Figure 2).

Row 4, Unit 1: Two threads are sticking out of the purple bead. Take the lower, bottom one and string 1 pink bead, pass this thread to the other side of the beadwork and up through the first red bead. String 1 pink bead. Pass the other, upper thread back through this last pink bead. As you tighten the threads, the beadwork should curl itself upward into a small squarish ball at the end.

Units 2–10: Pass the right thread upward through a red bead, the left thread up through a purple. Use one thread (it doesn't matter which) to string 1 pink bead, and pass the other thread back through this bead.

Unit 11: As in Units 2–10, pass the threads up through the red and purple beads. On the left thread, string 1 pink bead. Don't pass the right line back through this bead. Instead, tie a square knot—left over right, right over left—then pass the left thread back through the pink bead. Pull on the left thread a bit to tug the knot inside the pink bead, and then pull both threads to make sure the knot is tight. Pass the threads back down through the next red and purple beads, and then pass the left thread through the second-to-the-last pink bead. This time tie a surgeon's knot—left over right, right over left over left—and pass the left thread back through the pink bead. This knot will be a bit harder to pull inside the pink bead, but do your best. Tighten it as hard as you can, then clip the ends.

STEP 3: Remove the masking tape. String the crow bead over both ends of the lacing and push it upward to snug the bead tube fairly close to the key ring. Placing the tail ends of the lacing parallel to each other, tie a large overhand knot to keep the crow bead in place.

Figure 2. Row 4

Clovers and Ovals Necklace

This necklace is great practice for stringing beads with either hand, using beading wire instead of a needle and thread. By varying the types of beads you can coordinate it with everything from casual to couture.

MATERIALS

- 80 size 6° seed beads
- Size 10° seed beads, 2 strands
- 1½ yd size .014 or .019 49-strand beading wire
- 2 sterling silver 6mm split rings
- Small sterling silver lobster clasp or spring ring clasp
- Sterling silver 3 × 5mm jump ring
- 2 sterling silver 2 × 2mm crimp tubes
- 8 × 8" beading mat
- Masking tape
- Chain-nose pliers
- Wooden toothpick or round-nosed pliers
- Light-duty wire cutter

STEP 1: String 1 split ring then fold the wire so that both ends are together and the ring is in the middle. Holding both wire ends together as one, string 1 size 6° bead, crimp, and 1 size 6° bead. Slide these down to the split ring, leaving a tiny loop so that the split ring can swing a bit. Use the pliers to flatten the crimp bead.

STEP 2: On each end of the wire, string 10 size 10° seed beads. Do this by spreading the seed beads in a small area on your beading mat, and picking them up with an end of the wire in each hand. You'll probably be surprised to discover that, with a bit of practice, you can manage this even with your non-dominant hand. Finish this step by stringing 1 size 6° bead on one wire (now called Wire A), and passing the other wire end (Wire B) back through this bead while you hold the wire ends and the bead in your fingertips just as you would while tying an overhand knot. Once the incoming Wire B has passed back through the bead, pinch it between the thumb and forefinger of the hand opposite the one originally holding this wire (Hand A, Figure 1 on page 30), then use Hand B to pick up the end of Wire A. In other words, cross the

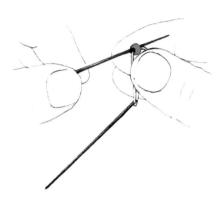

Figure 1. Pinch the crossing bead to keep the thread tight at the bottom on the bead hole.

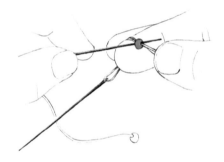

Figure 2. Drape thread over index finger and hold in place with middle finger and thumb.

> **TIP**
>
> *As mentioned in the "Basics" chapter, when using two needles to add one row alongside another, first do the pass through of the bead on the adjacent row, and then string the new beads on the other needle. Working this way makes it easier to decipher stripes and color changes. The South starting bead and the pass-through bead are known quantities, so get them out of the way first; then, you only have to deal with two beads. I use both hands to get the needle through an adjacent pass-through bead.*

wire ends over from one hand to the other with your thumb and fingertips. Pull the ends of the wire in opposite directions to tighten this oval at the center of the wire (Figure 2).

STEP 3: On each wire end, string 1 size 6° seed bead. On one wire, string another size 6° bead, and pass the other wire end back through this bead. Pull both wire ends to tighten.

STEP 4: Alternate Step 2 (ovals) and Step 3 (clovers) until you have 18 clovers. Use the masking tape to fasten the end of your chain to your work surface so that it doesn't flip around as you work.

STEP 5: String 10 size 10's on each wire. Hold both wire ends together as one and string 1 size 6° seed bead, 1 crimp bead, and 1 size 6° bead. Pull these beads down fairly close to the size 10's. Pass both ends back through the last bead strung, the crimp tube, and next 6° bead to form a loop. One at a time, carefully pull the wire ends to tighten this loop. When the loop is small enough, insert the toothpick or one tip of the round-

nosed plier to prevent the loop from being pulled through the beads. Holding the toothpick or round-nosed pliers horizontally, let the chain hang so that you can check the tightness. Pull on the wire ends to tighten if necessary. When you're satisfied with the drape of the chain, flatten the crimp tube with the pliers. Make sure you do a good, tight job of this, because this crimp tube is what will hold your chain together.

Use the wire cutters to trim the wire ends as close as you can to the hole on the size 6°—don't leave sharp, little ends that will prick your neck when you wear your necklace.

STEP 6: Use the oval jump ring to attach the clasp to the final wire loop.

MORE PRACTICE WORKING WITH NEEDLES

Return to the Rainbow Lanyard project. This time, instead of using monofilament, work through this project using a yard of 10lb test PowerPro with a size 10 beading needle threaded on each end and 6" thread tails. (Cutting and threading PowerPro is described in the "Materials and Tools" chapter.)

I'm adamant about using PowerPro for this exercise, because (unlike Nymo, for instance) it will not easily slip out of your needles—you can let the needle dangle and not worry about it falling off the thread, even when the tails are fairly short. Once you're an expert at managing two needles you can use any thread you please, but for this initial exercise, make it easy for yourself.

After you string your starting bead, hold both needles with one hand while the other hand pulls the bead to the center of the line. While the needles are still in the one hand, check to make sure both thread tails are about the same length.

CROSSING THREADS

Attempting to cross threads through a bead while it is still on the needle is an excellent way to draw blood. The crossing bead must be pulled off the end of the stringing needle before you pass the other needle back through it. The stringing needle is temporarily allowed to dangle after the crossing bead has been pulled off the needle end. Figures 3 and 4 show two methods for keeping the thread tight against the bottom of the crossing bead so it doesn't lie in the path of the incoming crossing needle.

Pass back through the crossing bead with the other needle. When this needle is halfway through the crossing bead, grasp its tip between your thumb and side of your index finger (of the hand that's holding the crossing bead). This allows you to release the needle end from your other hand, which then picks up the dangling stringing needle. This maneuver magically crosses the threads and exchanges the needles from one hand to the other. Pull the needles in opposite directions to slide the crossing bead down to the beadwork, in the same manner as you would tighten an overhand knot.

Figure 3. Left hand assists the right needle. Poke the pass-through needle halfway through the bead then use the other hand to grasp the needle tip and pull the needle through the remainder of the way.

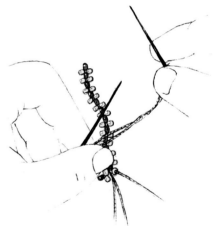

Figure 4. Left thumb holds work in place while right hand pulls the thread through the weave.

Chapter Four

Turns, Increases, Decreases

Most beaders have little difficulty learning to do

straight right-angle weave—it's when it comes time

to turn a corner and add another row that things seem

to get complicated. Fortunately, we have our four-bead

North-South-East-West compass diagram to help us navi-

gate these tricky spots. Relying on the compass diagram,

we consider each individual unit as a separate little

problem, and forget about thread paths. Concentrate

on the beads you need to string and to pass through,

and the thread path will take care of itself.

90° TURNS

The simplest turn is the 90° turn to the East or West. Those who worked through the Scoutmaster's Delight project are familiar with this one by now. They've also discovered that when using two needles, these turns are easy—simply decide whether it's an East or a West bead that the threads have to cross through, then string three beads on

Ninety-degree turns to the East and West

the opposite thread and cross threads through the last bead strung. It's rather like skiing—plant your pole, then make an arc with your skis to crank yourself around to the new direction. If you're turning to the East, the right-hand thread gets "planted," while the left-hand thread strings all three West, North, and East (crossing) beads. In the same fashion, when turning West, the

Two-needle 90° turn to the East

left thread sits idly by while the right thread strings the East, North, and West beads, then left makes a little move to pass back through the West bead.

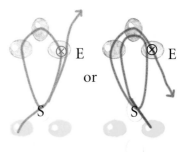

Single-needle 90° turns to the East

When using a single needle, sometimes your luck is with you and your clockwise or counterclockwise unit is in the same direction as the turn, so you simply have to string three beads and pass again through your starting bead and the first bead strung. Sometimes, alas, you have to string three beads, pass again through the starting bead, and then once more again through all three beads: two extra pass throughs; oh, the agony! Fortunately, however, this really doesn't require more advance planning than figuring out at the start of the turn whether

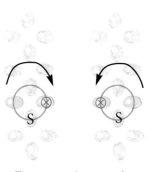

Turns connecting row ends

it's the East or West bead that the thread has to emerge from. Once you've strung the three new beads and passed through the South starting bead again, just keep circling on around until you come out where you want to be—East or West.

Connecting the two ends of a row is actually a simple 90° turn. The only difference is that the North bead is a pass through of the bead at the start of the chain, so the stringing sequence is: new bead, pass through, new bead. Again, determine at the start whether you want the crossing bead to be East or West, and everything will fall into place.

In the same manner, a 90° turn at the end of a row worked alongside another follows the same procedure, the only difference being a pass through (East or West) of one of the three turn beads. The stringing sequence is either: 1) pass through, new bead, new bead (two needles, or a single-needle clockwise turn); or, new bead, new bead, pass through (single needle doing a clockwise turn).

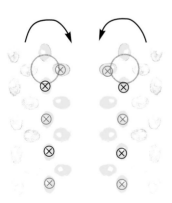

Turns at ends of rows

180° TURNS

For many, the truly confusing turn is the 180° turn required to start a new row alongside another. *This turn is merely a sequence of two identical 90° turns.* Simply concentrate on the four-bead compass pattern for each of the two units, and you'll emerge unscathed at the start of the new row.

For example, let's say you've made one row long enough, and want to end it and add a new row along the right-hand side. First, *end your row with a 90° turn* to the East, where you will have your crossing bead. *Rotate your beadwork* so that the crossing bead from this turn is now the South starting bead for the next unit. Now *make another 90° turn* to the East. *Rotate your work* so that the crossing bead from this last unit is in the South position ready for the next unit. Voilá! You've accomplished your 180° turn.

The four steps in a 180° turn, in a handy list:

STEP 1: End your row with a 90° turn to East or West.

STEP 2: Rotate your work so that the crossing bead from the last turn is now the South starting bead for the next unit.

STEP 3: Stitch another 90° turn in the same direction as the first.

STEP 4: Rotate your work so that the crossing bead from the last turn is now the South starting bead for the next unit.

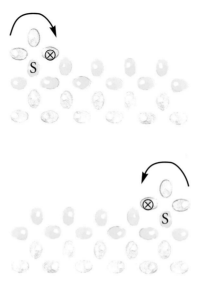

previous one, end your row with a standard 90° turn, rotate your work, and do the next 90° turn stringing two beads instead of three.

ONE-UNIT-SHORT DECREASE Steeper than the minus-1 decrease—just make your 180° turn one unit short of the end of the adjacent row.

Decrease by turning one weave short from end of row, at the second pass-through bead from the row end

Ninety-degree turns to the right or left at the start of a row; step three in a 180° turn

DECREASES AND INCREASES

MINUS-1 DECREASE The minus-1 decrease is simply Step 3 in a 180° turn sequence, minus one bead. Instead of three beads (East, North, West) required to make the turn, one bead gets eliminated. Thus to make the next row slightly shorter than the

The minus-1 decrease

STANDARD AND GRADUAL INCREASES OR DECREASES

These are often encountered when tailoring the beadwork to cover a form. They're very intuitive: to increase, string two beads on either the East or West instead of one; to decrease, pass through two beads on either the East or West; to decrease, pass through two beads of the previous row on either the East or the West instead of one. As increases and decreases tend to create the appearance of little holes in the bead mesh, also shown is a more gradual method of constructing the increases or decreases over the course of 2 rows instead of 1, which helps to minimize the effect of these holes.

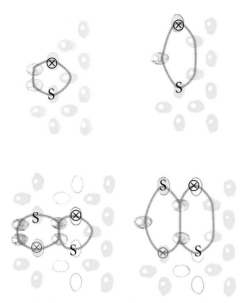

Standard increase; standard decrease; gradual increase over two rows; gradual decrease over two rows

FLOATING UNITS Most often used when working curved rows, these are gap-filling units. Normally when working alongside another row, the thread passes through an adjacent bead to the East or West; however, with a floating unit there is no pass through or attachment to the previous row—the unit just "floats."

Floating increase—no pass through of an adjacent bead in the prior row

FIGURE-EIGHT INCREASES AND DECREASES

Now that you've mastered turns, we'll consider figure-eight increases and decreases. Use these when a new row is to be longer or shorter than the previous one—for instance, when working adjacent rows to make a triangular or circular piece of beadwork. In the sample pieces in this book

- figure-eight *increases* are worked *horizontally*, at the *start* of a new row, whereas
- figure-eight *decreases* are worked *vertically*, at the *end* of a row.

Decreases take a bit of advance planning, as they occur before the last beads on the adjacent row.

While it's easy to visualize a figure-eight unit in a diagram, it's less easy to recognize when actually working it while the beads are all lying askew. It doesn't fall into place until the very last cross-through. So, to match the diagrams, I've listed the bead-by-bead working sequences for figure-eight units. The figure-eight may be puzzling when you first encounter it. Once you understand it, though, it's very handy for maneuvering and tailoring the beadwork.

Of course, you can also work figure-eight units by the "whoops" method: "Whoops! I went too far. Guess I'll just have to weave backwards a bit." This fills the bead holes with thread, but at least you don't have to unravel your work.

Two needles, figure-eight increase and turn to the East

STEP 1: Finish the prior row a turn to the East and rotate your work so the crossing bead is in the South position (Steps 1 and 2 of the 180° turn).

STEP 2: Use the left needle to string 4 beads and then pass through the first one again (West) to form the increase unit.

STEP 3: String North and East. Pass again through the South starting bead and the North and East.

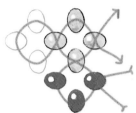

Figure-eight increase and turn to the East

Single needle, figure-eight increase and clockwise turn to the East

STEP 1: Finishing the prior row with Steps 1 and 2 of the 180° sequence has resulted in a clockwise turn coming up: your thread is exiting the West side of the South starting bead.

STEP 2: String 4 beads and then pass again through the first one again (West) to form the increase unit.

STEP 3 : String North and East. Pass again through the South starting bead and the North and East.

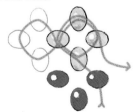

Single needle, figure-eight increase and clockwise turn to the East

Single needle, figure-eight increase and counterclockwise turn to the East

STEP 1: Finishing the prior row with Steps 1 and 2 of the 180° sequence has resulted in a counterclockwise turn coming up; your thread is exiting the East side of the South starting bead.

STEP 2: String 6 beads and pass through the third bead (West) to form the increase unit.

STEP 3: Pass again through the South starting bead and East.

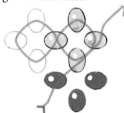

Single needle, figure-eight increase and counter clockwise turn to the East

Two needles, figure-eight increase and turn to the West

STEP 1: Finish the previous row with Steps 1 and 2 of the 180° turn sequence.

STEP 2: Use the right needle to string 4 beads and then pass through the first one again (East) to form the increase unit.

STEP 3: Use the right needle to string the

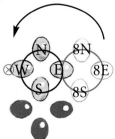

Figure-eight increase and turn to the left (West)

North and West beads. Pass back through the West bead with the right needle.

Single needle, figure-eight increase and clockwise turn to the West

STEP 1: Finishing the prior row with Steps 1 and 2 of the 180° sequence has resulted in a clockwise turn coming up; your thread is emerging from the West side of the South starting bead.

STEP 2: String 6 beads and pass again through the West.

STEP 3: Pass again through the South starting bead and the West.

Single needle, figure-eight increase and counterclockwise turn to the West

STEP 1: Finishing the prior row with Steps 1 and 2 of the 180° sequence has resulted in a counterclockwise turn coming up; your thread is emerging from the East side of the South starting bead.

STEP 2: String 4 beads and pass again through the East.

STEP 3: String North and West, pass again through the South starting bead and North and West.

Two needles, figure-eight decrease, turn to the East

STEP 1: Begin 3 units from the end of the adjacent row. Using the West thread:

▨ pass through the adjacent bead 1 on prior row

▨ string 3 beads, pass down through bead 2 on the adjacent row, and pass through the first bead strung

▨ string East crossing bead.

STEP 2: Pass the East thread back through the East bead.

Single needle, clockwise figure-eight decrease and turn to the East

Begin 3 units from the end of the adjacent row. With the thread emerging from the West side of the South starting bead:

STEP 1: Same as Step 1 above (two needles, figure-eight decrease, turn to the East).

STEP 2: Pass through the South starting bead, bead 1 of the adjacent row, the North, and the East.

Figure-eight decrease and turn to the East

Single needle, counterclockwise figure-eight decrease and turn to the East

Begin 3 units from the end of the adjacent row. With the thread emerging from the East side of the South starting bead:

STEP 1: String 2 beads and pass up through bead 2 on the adjacent row.

- string 2 beads: East and North
- pass through bead 2 on the adjacent row
- string North 2 and East 2
- pass through North again
- pass back down through bead 1 on adjacent row
- pass through South and East crossing bead

STEP 2: Pass through the South starting bead and the East.

Two needles, figure-eight decrease and turn to the West

STEP 1: Start 3 beads from the end of the adjacent row.

- Using the East thread:
- pass through the adjacent bead 1 on the prior row
- string 3 beads: North, West 2, North 2
- pass back down through bead 2 on the adjacent row
- pass through North again
- string the West crossing bead

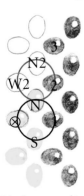

Figure-eight decrease and turn to the West

STEP 2: Pass the West thread back through the West bead.

Single needle, clockwise figure-eight decrease and turn to the West

Start 3 beads from the end of the adjacent row.

With the thread exiting from the West side of the South starting bead:

- string 2 beads: West and North
- pass through bead 2 on the adjacent row
- string North 2 and West 2
- pass through North again
- pass back down through bead 1 on adjacent row
- pass through the South and West crossing bead

Single needle, counterclockwise figure-eight decrease and turn to the West

Begin 3 beads from the end of the adjacent row. With the thread exiting from the East side of the South starting bead:

- pass through the adjacent bead 1 on the prior row
- string 3 beads: North, East 2, North 2
- pass back down through bead 2 on the adjacent row
- pass through North again
- string the West crossing bead
- pass again through South, bead 1, North, and West

Chapter Five

Chains

Simple chains are ideal for

practicing right-angle weave. The

Jabot pattern requires much less

stitching through seed beads if done

with two needles, so try it if you would

like some extensive practice

using two needles.

Bead Lace Jabot

This lacy design can be worn as a jabot, or twisted
with another scarf to add some beady zest.

Figure 1. 11 × 1 chain

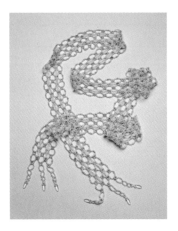

Multibead units offer texture and pattern excitement beyond the basic 1 × 1 unit. Different units can be mixed within a row; for example, the 1 × 1 and 11 × 1 units in the "clovers and ovals" pattern (Figure 1).

STEP 1: Work three 60" clovers and ovals chains—an alternating sequence of 1 × 1 short and 11 × 1 long units, beginning and ending with whatever sequence you fancy for the 2–3" fringe tails on the ends of the chains (Figure 2). Position a 3mm or 4mm bead in the middle of the 11 beads in the 11 × 1 long unit (string 5 seed beads, 1 large bead, and 5 seed beads).

These larger beads serve as connection points for joining the chains together. **Note:** When you're working the chains, be careful not to skip the 1 × 1 short units. It's easy to get carried away stringing the correct number of seed beads for the long units, and to forget about the 1 × 1 units. Having to snip threads and weave in the correct unit is very aggravating.

STEP 2: Connect the chains with rows of 1 × 1 units, working five seed bead units between the fire-polished connection beads at the centers of the ovals (see Figure 3).

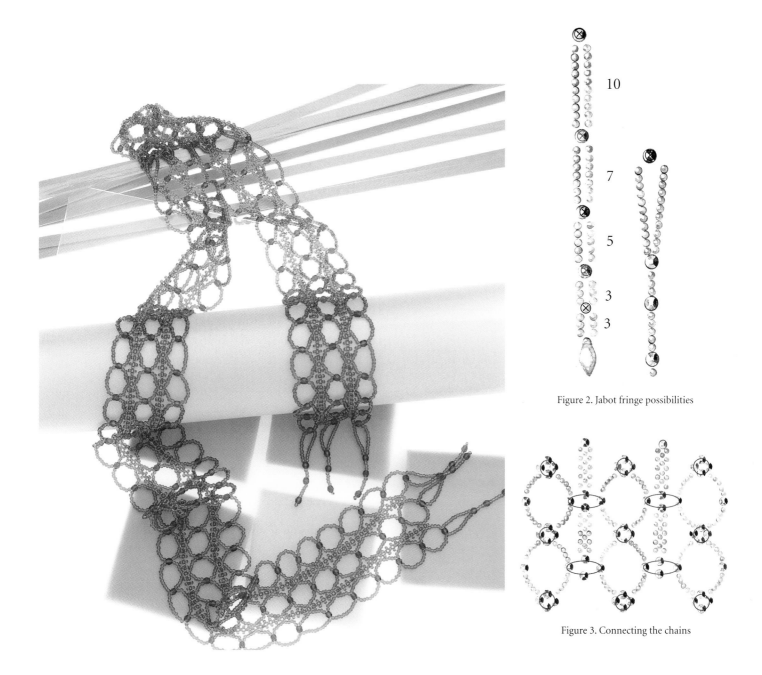

Figure 2. Jabot fringe possibilities

10

7

5

3

3

Figure 3. Connecting the chains

Carnelian and Garnet Necklace

Laden with the rich hues of orange and scarlet, this necklace is special enough to appear with your most elegant outfit . . . and on the cover of this book!

MATERIALS

- *Five 16" strands of 6mm faceted carnelian rondelles*
- *Two 16" strands of 4mm round purple garnet beads*
- *Seven 16" strands of 2mm round purple garnet beads*
- *PowerPro 10lb test (avoid nylon thread)*
- *Size 12 needle(s)*
- *Size 15 needle for small bead holes*

---

3 × 1 RIBBONS

When you're weaving beads with sharp edges such as lead glass crystals or gemstone beads, "in between" beads can be used as thread covers to minimize the thread rubbing against the sharp sides of the bead holes. The result resembles a 1 × 1 unit, but is actually 3 × 1. There are two variations: 1) a small/large/small bead trio for each East and West, then a large bead for the crossing bead; 2) a large/small/large bead trio for each East and West, then a small bead for the crossing bead.

In the first variation, the large beads form the South-East-West-North compass pattern, and are the working beads through which the thread crossing and pass throughs are done(Figure 1); in the second, the small beads are the working beads (see Figure 1, page 48).

STEP 1: String a 4mm garnet as the starting bead, then weave a 24" ribbon of two rows of 3 × 1 units of 6mm carnelian rondelles and 2mm round garnet beads. End the last unit of Row 2 with a 4mm garnet in the North position.

Figure 1. 3 × 1 units

STEP 2: Place the ribbon ends together at a right angle. Begin a new thread join with a row of 3 × 1 units of 4mm garnet and 2mm garnet beads, then continue as a new row along the inside edge to the middle of the back (Figure 2).

STEP 3: Start another row of 4mm and 2mm garnets and continue it around the outside edge to the middle back. Check all your knots to ensure they're concealed tightly inside the beads, then trim the thread ends.

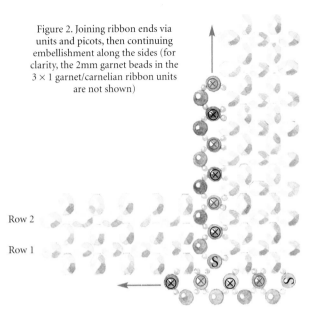

Figure 2. Joining ribbon ends via units and picots, then continuing embellishment along the sides (for clarity, the 2mm garnet beads in the 3 × 1 garnet/carnelian ribbon units are not shown)

Row 2

Row 1

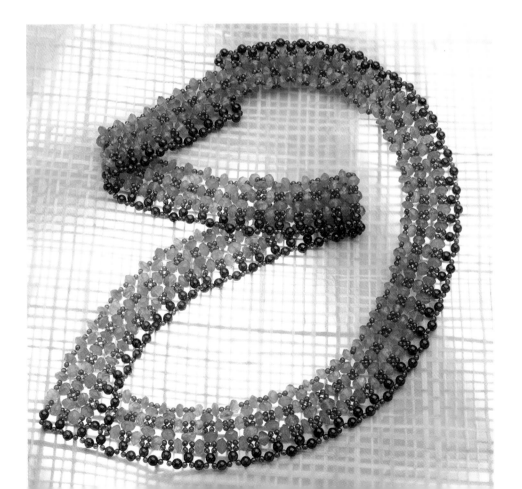

Sapphire Crystals Bracelet

Delicate and dainty, this bracelet will add a mischievous
touch of sparkle to your suits, jeans, or dressiest dresses.

MATERIALS

72 Swarovski 4mm bicones in a mix of sapphire AB, capri blue, and capri blue AB

72 Swarovski 4mm bicones in clear crystal

Size 10° Czech turquoise white heart seed beads

10 size 10° Czech crystal luster seed beads

Strong silver magnetic clasp

2 oval silver jump rings

2 yd PowerPro 10lb test, or 3 yd of your preferred thread for a single needle

Size 10 or 12 beading needle(s)

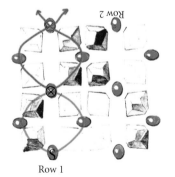

Figure 1. Sapphire crystal bracelet pattern

Following the pattern (Figure 1), weave a
row of 18 units for the 7½" bracelet pictured.

The 180° turn with the seed-bead loop
between Rows 1 and 2 is a bit tricky. With
two needles the sequence is:

STEP 1:   For the last unit on Row 1, the
West thread strings 1 crystal, 1 seed bead,
crystal, 1 seed bead, 1 blue crystal, 1 seed
bead; the East thread strings 1 blue crystal

and crosses through the last seed bead on
the West thread.

STEP 2:   Rotate your work 90° so that the
crossing seed bead from the last unit is in
the South position.

STEP 3:   To make the bead loop, the West
thread strings 1 blue crystal, 1 seed bead, 5
crystal luster seed beads, passes through the

North seed bead and blue crystal from the previous unit, and then passes through the first blue crystal strung and the seed bead. This thread then strings 1 crystal, 1 seed bead, 1 crystal, and the crossing seed bead.

STEP 4: The East thread strings 1 crystal and passes back through the last seed bead on the other thread.

STEP 5: Rotate the work 90° so that the crossing seed bead from the last unit is in the South position at the base of Row 2.

When you're using a single needle, the clockwise-counterclockwise circling complicates the thread path a bit. Depending upon which way you're circling, complete the last unit of Row 1 with the thread exiting from the East seed bead. Rotate your work so that this bead is in the South position. Depending on which side of the seed bead your thread is exiting, follow the thread path in the diagram to work the loop. Continue around until you've completed the starting unit at the base of Row 2, with the thread exiting from the indicated crossing bead. Rotate the work 90° so that this final crossing seed bead is in the South position at the base of Row 2 (Figure 2).

The ending loop follows a similar progression, starting from the final crossing seed bead in the North position at the last unit. The diagram shows a knot inside one of the blue crystals. However, if you're following a different color arrangement, pick whichever crystal color you think is most likely to conceal the knot. Trim the thread ends (Figure 3).

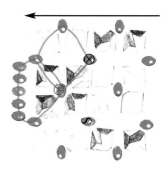

Figure 2. Loop at turns between Rows 1 and 2

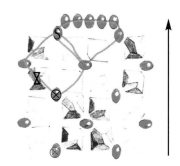

Figure 3. Loop at the end

Chapter Six

Fabric Effects

Because of its flexibility,

right-angle weave is often used

to cover objects, and can be tailored

to fit. Or, create a fabric that can

be used all on its own.

Ruffle Bracelet

This bracelet flutters with color . . . play with
different hues to personalize it for your wardrobe.

MATERIALS

▨ *Size 10° Czech transparent orange and white opal seed beads*

▨ *Plastic "Moonglow" beads from a 1960s necklace, graduated from 6.5 to 14mm*

▨ *Bar and ring toggle clasp*

▨ *Two oval jump rings*

▨ *White PowerPro 10lb test*

▨ *Needle(s)*

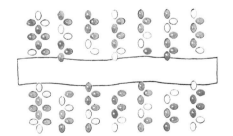

Figure 1. Chevron pattern for ruffles bracelet ribbon

Use large beads of any size. You don't have
to attach a clasp—this design also works
beautifully when strung with elastic.

STEP 1: See Figure 1. Make a ribbon of 1
× 1 units, seven rows of stripes forming a
chevron pattern. The chevrons will help you
find the spots to pass the needle through to
form an even ruffle. This sample ribbon is
14" long. For a ruffle that completely encir-
cles a wrist, try a ribbon 22" long. Or use
smaller accent beads so the ruffle doesn't
have to be as deep.

STEP 2: This bracelet was strung using a
doubled yard of PowerPro, starting with a
loop of 5 beads, then 3 accent beads with a
white opal spacer bead between each of
them. Start the ruffle by passing the needle
and thread downward through the ribbon
in the middle of one end, through the hole
in a center of a unit. Note the position of this
unit in relation to the first white chevron
stripe where the needle enters the ribbon.
Skipping one stripe, stitch upwards through
the ribbon at the same unit position in relation to the white stripe as in the first stitch.

String a bead and, skipping a white stripe, stitch downward through the ribbon in the same relative unit position as in the first stitch, then skip a stripe, and stitch upward, again in the same spot relative to the white stripe. As you tighten the thread, the ribbon will fold into a ruffle. If you are using graduated beads as in the sample, you may have to skip two white stripes in the center instead of just one, to accommodate the extra width of the center bead. The ribbon should surround the bottom half of the bead. That is, the needle exit and entry points that form the fold around the bottom of the bead should be at the same level as the bead's holes.

STEP 3: End with the 3 accent beads and 5-bead loop, then pass back through the beads and tie an overhand knot after each of the first 2 accent beads (separating the two threads and pulling them in opposite directions will magically tighten this knot close to the bead). After passing back through the third accent bead, work the threads in opposite directions through a few of the 1 × 1 units of the ruffle fabric, tying concealed square knots as you go. End with a concealed surgeon's knot, then trim the thread ends.

STEP 4: Use the oval jump rings to attach the clasp to the bead loops.

Party Purse

My husband happened upon a purse like this at a garage sale, and he knew I'd love it! There are many ways to update this classic design: use smaller beads for a tiny amulet bag or an evening wrist purse; create lattice effects by substituting a 2 × 2 unit instead of 1 × 1, or by using a 3 × 1 unit with bugles and seed beads . . . not to mention the endless color and texture possibilities.

MATERIALS

- *2,328 plastic 6mm faceted beads (fuchsia AB)*
- *10lb test monofilament line*
- *Thread*
- *Purse handles*
- *Needle(s)*

STEP 1: Follow the dimensions in the diagram on page 56 to construct three connected rectangles: 33 × 13, 21 × 20, and 15 × 7. Tie a marker thread to each of the 2 beads on the outside of the 3rd and 31st units in the 33-unit base row.

STEP 2: Fold the purse and attach the side flaps to the body with another row of units. Start each connecting row at the out-side edges of the widest rectangle and work down the sides and then across the bottom. End with a knot inside a bead in the purse body. You'll be doing further weaving through the beads at the purse top edge, so you don't want to fill them with thread or knots.

STEP 3: For the purse handle, work a 37 × 4 four-sided tube in the same manner as the

Rainbow Lanyard (page 25): 3 rows plus a final 4th row that zips Row 3 to Row 1.

STEP 4: To connect the handle to the purse, fold the purse's sides in, with each fold centered on the marked bead. For each side, consider this bead as "South." Center a thread through this bead and, using two needles to work 2 units, connect the sides of the fold (pass through East, pass through West, string North on one thread and cross the other thread through it). Work 1 unit upward to connect to one of the end units on the handle (Figure 1). (String an East and a West,

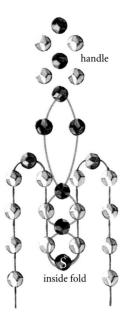

Figure 1. Top edge of purse

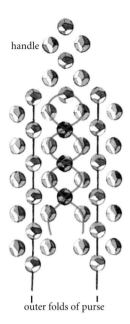

handle

outer folds of purse

Figure 2. Side of the purse

cross through a bead on the handle end as North.) For the 4th unit, pass each thread through the East or West side beads at the base of the handle, and weave a downward picot to connect the handle sides to the fold sides (string 1 bead, pass through the bead on the top edge of the fold, string 1 bead, and pass through the East or West again). Cross through the "North bead" on the opposite side of the handle, then work one unit down (pass through East and West, string a North bead and cross the other thread through it). Work 3 more units down the outside of the purse (pass through East and West, string a new North crossing bead), connecting the outer edges

of the fold (Figure 2). Tie as many knots as will make you feel confident the fold won't pull apart.

STEP 5: Make a 12-bead cube (see page 72), and attach it to the purse front seven beads down from the top center edge (at Unit 11).

STEP 6: Center a 9-bead loop at Unit 8 of the purse flap, to fit over the bead cube for closure.

STEP 7: Check to be sure all your knots are tight and trim thread ends.

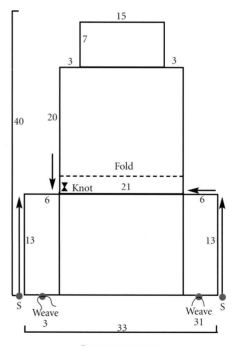

Party purse pattern

BUT WAIT! THERE'S MORE!

Inside this purse was a nifty miniature purse keychain.

> ### MATERIALS
> - 45 6mm faceted round plastic beads
> - 12 4mm gold plastic beads
> - 4 flower shanked button beads
> - 10lb test monofilament
> - Keychain finding

STEP 1: Weave a 3 × 5 rectangle of 1 × 1 units (Figure 3), exiting the last unit on the West bead on the side. Rotate the work so that this bead is in the South position for the next unit.

STEP 2: Make a picot turn to the East to connect the two sides and to get into position to make the handle. Follow Figure 1 to string the handle (two threads are shown, but if you're using the single-needle method, of course you'll just use one thread).

STEP 3: Continue with 2 more units to close up the other side of the purse. Knot and trim the threads. Attach the keychain finding.

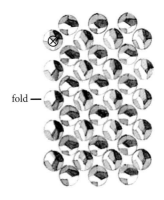

fold —

Figure 3. Mini-purse rectangle

Figure 4. Side closure and handle

Chapter Seven

The Triangle Tube

The versatile triangle tube takes

right-angle weave into three dimensions. Its

close cousin, the box chain, is an easy way to con-

struct a perfectly square tube (see the Rainbow

Lanyard as an example). Depending upon the size

and mix of the beads used, the triangle tube can

form beads, bracelets, bangles, and long flexible

chains. Its edges can be reinforced to form bars

and circles. And oddly enough, it doesn't

resemble a triangle at all.

The Lei Bracelet

Delightfully supple and flexible, this is a good project for beginners. It can be a simple, random blend of colors, or made more challenging by incorporating a spiral stripe. However, the festive mix of opaque and transparent colors seems to be the key to its appeal. As with the Rainbow Lanyard, it can also be worked without needles, using 10lb test monofilament.

MATERIALS

- *260 size 6° seed beads, mixed matte opaque and transparent colors*
- *8' of PowerPro 10lb test*
- *Size 10 beading needle(s)*
- *Glue*

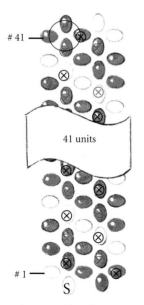

Figure 1. Lei bracelet pattern

The pattern includes a stripe if you wish to try it. A triangle weave can accommodate a spiral of three different colors, but for the lei bracelet a combination of two matte opaque stripes with one transparent seems to work out well, adding a bit of sparkle with a subtle underlying pattern (Figure 1).

STEP 1: To calculate the number of units you will need in the starting chain, multiply your wrist size in inches by forty-two and then divide by eight, round up from half, and subtract one. For an 8" bracelet, begin with a chain of 8" × 42 = 41 units plus a 90° turn to the East at the end. As instructed in the "Turns, Increases, and Decreases" on page 34, continue with another 90° turn to the East to get into position to work the second row. For the second row, pass through the East bead in each unit, and string new West and North beads. End with a 90° turn to the West.

STEP 2: Zip up your rows. Do so by rotating your beadwork to match Figure 2; with the thread(s) exiting from the now-East bead in the lower right-hand corner of the work. Zip up the first unit of the third row, by stringing a new South bead, passing through the West bead on the opposite side of the chain, and stringing a new North crossing bead (the sequence will be backwards for a counterclockwise single-needle unit). Continue to zip together the edges of the rows by passing through the respective East and West beads on opposite edges of the chain and then string a new North crossing bead. Success! You've created a triangle tube.

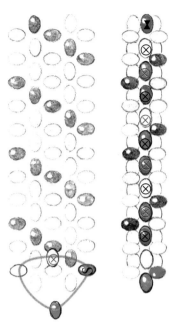

Figure 2. Zip-up row

STEP 3: Connect the tube ends. This can be confusing, so keep this sequence firmly in mind:

- The first joining unit strings 2 new beads
- The second joining unit strings 1 new bead
- The third joining unit strings no new beads at all.

To join the two ends:

Step 3a: Starting in the North position, string a new East bead, pass through the South at the opposite end of the chain at the beginning of Row 3, string a new West crossing bead (or just the reverse sequence for a counterclockwise single-needle unit, although the crossing is still done through the West bead). As you tighten the unit, the chain will curl into a circle (Figure 3).

Step 3b: Arrange the chain so the crossing bead is now in the South position for the next weave. If this bead seems to be in an inconvenient spot, roll the chain a bit to bring the bead into a more accessible position, either on the inside or the outside of the tube. Make sure the upcoming East and West beads are on either side of the gap between the ends of the tube, not the ones from the previous unit in Step 3a. Pass through East and West and string a new North crossing bead (Figure 4).

Step 3c: Starting in the South position, pass the thread around through the East, North, and West to close up the remainder of the gap, and then tie a knot (Figure 5). Work the thread back around through a unit or two and tie another knot. Dab glue on the knots.

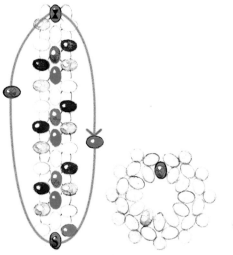

Figure 3. Connecting the ends Figure 4. Final unit Figure 5. Knotting the ends

Eyeglasses Leash

A triangle tube worked with size 11° or 10° seed beads makes a spunky eyeglasses leash. Try the three-color spiral pattern from the Lei Bracelet. If you don't have the little rubber ring findings for the ends of the leash, you can weave a sliding adjustable loop.

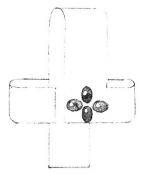

Figure 1. Adjustable loop

MATERIALS
- *2 strands size 11° or 10° seed beads*
- *30' of PowerPro 10lb test*
- *Size 10 beading needle(s)*

STEP 1: Pass a thread around through the three beads at the end of the tube and through a size 6° seed bead or 3mm or 4mm bead.

STEP 2: Work a chain of eight to twelve 1 × 1 units, exiting the last unit with a 90° turn to the East.

STEP 3: Work four or five 1 × 1 units, then *fold the first chain over* and circle the small chain around it, working a final unit to connect to the West bead at the end of the first chain (Figure 1).

STEP 4: Work the thread back through the first chain and knot inside the larger bead between the loop and the leash. Glue liberally, but don't get any glue on the chain that loops around, or it won't be very adjustable.

Torus Beads

These beaded donut beads are made the same as the Lei Bracelet, but shorter.

MATERIALS

▨ *Size 6° seed beads, mixed matte opaque and transparent colors*

▨ *3' of PowerPro 10lb test*

▨ *Size 10 beading needle(s)*

STEP 1: Make a short 11-bead row, working Rows 2 and 3 to create a triangle tube, and then connect the ends to form a circle.

STEP 2: Arrange the tube so that the flat triangular base is on the outside and the point on the inside, and you have a Torus bead. Accentuate the outside rims by stringing reinforcing beads between each rim bead.

Wreath Beads

Wreath beads are great to string on your creations
as accent beads, or stunning as stand-alone focal beads.

MATERIALS

- *Size 6° and 11° seed beads and fringe drop beads*
- *4mm and 3mm round fire-polished beads*
- *PowerPro 10lb test*
- *Size 10 or 12 beading needle(s)*

Make a Torus bead, but work in a 3 × 1 unit instead of 1 × 1. The 3-bead stringing sequence is small/large/small. Imagine the small beads serving as covers for the thread connecting the large "working" beads in a 1 × 1 unit. As the work proceeds, these small beads will form tiny four-leaf clover patterns.

NOTES

The addition of the small beads not only conceals the thread, but also opens the weave to accommodate drop beads around the outside. Use the drops as the South and North beads in Row 1, and you won't have to add them later when connecting the ends of the triangle tube to form the circle (they'll be East and West pass-through beads during the tube ends connection).

In the samples using 4mm faceted beads, smaller 3mm beads were used for the West beads in Row 2, to accommodate the smaller circumference of the inner ring of the bead.

The Right-Angle Bangle

This is an inside-out Lei Bracelet or Torus Bead—the triangles point outward like a flying saucer. The outer edge is reinforced with beads slightly smaller than those used to construct the bracelet, and the inner two edges are reinforced with even smaller seed beads. These added beads stiffen the slinky Lei Bracelet into a bangle.

MATERIALS

- *220 4mm round faceted fire-polished beads*
- *36 3mm round faceted fire-polished beads*
- *Size 9° three-cut beads, or size 10° seed beads*
- *PowerPro 10lb test*
- *Size 12 beading needle(s)*

Triangle tube cross sections

STEP 1: Multiply the wrist measurement (in inches) by 35 and then divide by 7½ to determine the number of units needed in the first row. The number of beads ratio formula is similar: 220 times (the wrist diameter in inches) divided by 7½.

STEP 2: Follow the same procedure as in the lei bracelet for turns, Rows 2 and 3, for creating the circular triangle tube. Work with a relaxed but firm thread tension throughout—don't try to pull the thread so tightly the beads squeak. Too tight a weave will also cause difficulties later when adding the 3mm beads. Tie one square knot inside either an East or West bead on the last circle connection unit, and don't trim the thread—we'll be using it to add the 3mm beads.

STEP 3: Roll the tube so that the inside of the bracelet is flat, and the thread is exiting from a bead along the outer spine edge. Pass around through the spine, stringing a 3mm bead between each 4mm bead. Tie a concealed knot when finished.

STEP 4: Start a new thread, and string a seed bead between each 4mm bead along the two inside edges (work the thread through a unit when finished circling one edge in order to start the other). Tie a concealed knot and trim the ends. Apply glue to the knots if you wish.

The sample variations include:

- Substituting size 6°, 8°, and 10° beads for the 4mm, 3mm, and 9° three-cuts.
- Embellishing the outer two sides with floret beads or stone chips.
- Creating a "caged beads" effect by stringing 36 round 3mm round beads, placing them inside the triangle tube before zipping it up, and then tying them into a circle with a hidden square knot before Units 2 and 3 of the closure.
- The pearl bangle was done with a 3 × 1 small/large/small unit and the finished circular triangle tube arranged as a bangle, with the triangular point on the outer edge. No reinforcing beads were needed.

Bangle outside and inside edges reinforcement

1920s Coral Necklace and Earrings

Classic and stunning, this subtle piece embodies timeless elegance. And the bonus is that it's very comfortable to wear.

MATERIALS

- *580 round 3mm beads for necklace, 65 for each earring ball*
- *500 round 4mm beads*
- *2 round 10mm beads*
- *Silk twist*
- *Bell bead caps*
- *Two-strand box clasp*
- *Two head pins*
- *Earring findings of your choice*

NECKLACE

STEP 1: There are two different approaches to the construction of this necklace: Version 1: Make two triangle tubes, 82 beads by 15½" (40 cm) long, one of 3mm and one of 4mm beads. Connect them with 3mm beads; Version 2: Make a 3-row ribbon of beads, 82 beads by 15½" (40 cm) long, graduated from 3mm for Row 1, three 3mm and one 4mm for Row 2, and 4mm for Row 3, and then build a triangle tube atop Rows 1 and 3. The latter method is more appropriate for gemstone beads, as it allows you to achieve a subtle curvature with graduated beads in approximate sizes. You can conceal the more flawed beads in the base ribbon, saving the best beads for the top front. **Note:** The curvature of the necklace shown was accommodated by graduating the beads and by stringing two beads to connect the 4mm tube to the clasp versus only one for the 3mm tube.

STEP 2: Attach one of the tubes to the clasp by passing separate threads through each of the 3 terminal beads at the ends of the triangle tubes, the bead cap, and through a clasp loop. Pass back through all several times and knot and glue the threads inside the bell caps.

EARRINGS

STEP 1: Start a ball by weaving a 7 × 3-unit rectangle of beads.

STEP 2: Work one short connecting row at a right angle to close it into a ring, exiting from a bead at the side.

Pass a thread through the 8 beads at the edge of the ring to draw it together into a cup.

STEP 3: Cap one end of the bead with a 2 × 1 unit connected to the opposite side of the cup (the North crossing bead is on the other side of the cup), and then work the thread(s) through the ring to its other side.

STEP 4: Insert a 10mm bead and work the thread around the ringed edge to draw it together into a cup.

STEP 5: Place a 3mm bead on a head pin and pass through the middle of the 4 beads in the bottom 2 × 1 cap unit and through the interior bead. Work a final 2 × 1 unit to form the top cap around the head pin. Use round-nose pliers to make a loop in the head pin and attach the beaded bead to your earring.

Chapter Eight

Cubes

What's a more natural thing to

make with a four-directional weave than

a cube? Cubic beads make wonderful

counterpoints to rounded beads or design

elements. Because right-angle weave is so

flexible, however, the trick is to get the

cube to stay nice and crisp instead of

resembling a squishy, wet cardboard

box. Here are three ways to do it.

Twelve-Bead Cube

Sinfully easy to make, these are a great way to use up your bead odds
and ends, or to make coordinated accents for your designs.

MATERIALS

- *12 beads*
- *2' monofilament line, or PowerPro with a needle threaded onto each end*
- *Optional: 8 seed beads for corner embellishment*

STEP 1: String 1 bead and center it on the thread. *String 1 bead onto each thread end. String 1 more bead on one thread, and then cross the other thread through this bead.* Repeat between ** two more times to make a 3-unit chain.

STEP 2: String 1 bead on each thread, then cross the threads through the very first bead at the base of the chain (Figure 1). As you pull the thread ends to tighten them, the chain will curl up into a cube. I find it helps the cube keep its shape to back one thread out of the first/last bead, tie a square knot, and then run the thread back through the bead. Pull the square knot to reposition it inside the bead and to tighten the cube.

STEP 3: Pass each thread around through the four beads on each side of the cube, and then knot them as above inside a center bead. *Optional:* To accentuate the corners of the cube, string a seed bead at each corner as you pass the threads around each side (Figure 2).

BONUS TIP
If you use droplet beads, the result is a twelve-pointed star bead cluster.

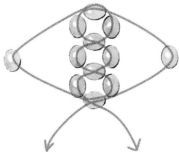

Figure 1. Cube stringing

Figure 2. Cube corner embellishment

Bead in a Box

Although not rigid enough to stand all on its own, this design
works superbly as a cover for a large bicone or cube bead; or, fill
it with packing pearls, lightweight plastic beads, or batting.

MATERIALS

- Size 10° seed beads: crystal for cube faces, transparents for face centers, white opal for face sides, white for cube edges
- 22mm acrylic bicone bead
- PowerPro 10lb test
- Size 10 beading needle(s)

Because we have to watch out for the corner units, our sample uses white beads for the edges of the cube so that you can tell which beads belong to the edges and which to the faces.

STEP 1: Make two 5 × 17 rectangles, each comprised of three 5 × 5-unit cube faces separated by white East and West hinge rows.

STEP 2: Attach the end of one rectangle to the center edge of the other by working a hinge row, adding white North and South crossing beads (Figure 1). Note that the cube corner units are made up of only three beads. To make a corner, pass through a white hinge bead, then string a white North crossing bead and continue the edge row to connect the next pair of faces.

STEP 3: Continue the hinge row around to connect the faces along one side of the cube, and then work across and down one face to zip together the other three faces. Insert the bicone bead before you completely zip together the last edge. To finish, tie two concealed knots. Trim the thread ends.

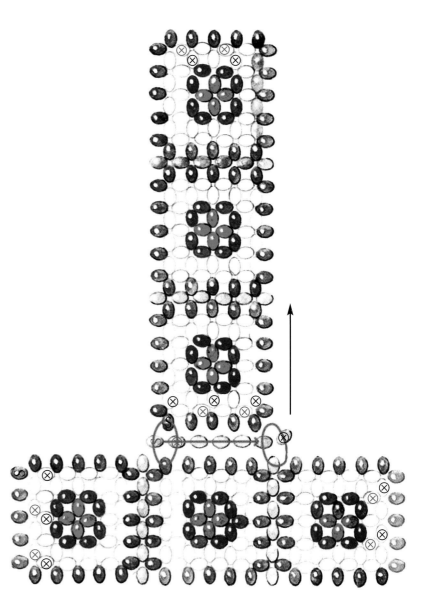

Figure 1. Bead in a box pattern

Sugar Cubes

These nifty little gems are as addicting as potato chips—you can't make just one. Like tablets, they're a fun way to experiment with transparency and color blends. A mat of five squares is folded like an accordion, and then the edges are zipped together. The trick to navigating the zip-up sequence around the four sides of the cube is to keep rotating your work to maintain the South-to-North orientation for each unit.

MATERIALS

- *Czech 10° seed beads:*
  Crystal luster (or other light transparent) for two sides
  White opaque to outline the two transparent sides
  3 opaque colors
  White opal for the "hinges" and zip-up units
- **Two needles:**
  - *2 yd of PowerPro 10lb test for mat and sides 1 and 2; 18" of PowerPro 10lb test for sides 3 and 4*
- **Single needle:**
  - *3 yd of whatever thread you prefer and 1 yd for sides 3 and 4*

SUGAR CUBE PATTERN

STEP 1: Follow Figure 1 to make a mat that is 24 units long by 4 rows wide. In the sample, the first and last squares are trans-

parent, with three squares of opaque colors in the middle. When following the pattern, be careful to note where the opaque white beads appear at the edges of the two transparent sides (Colors 1 and 5). The

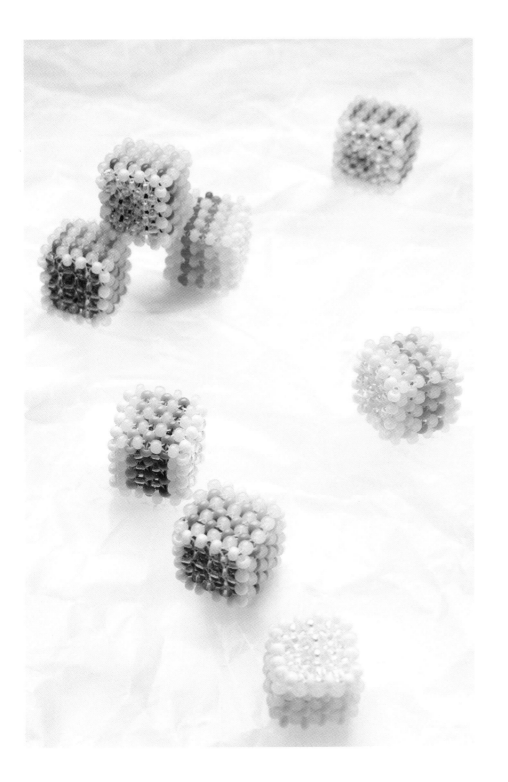

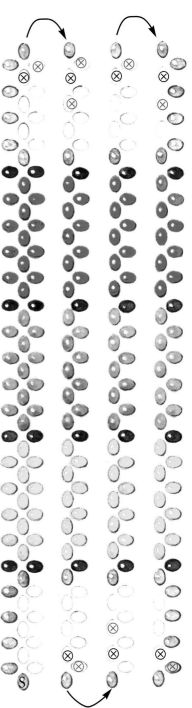

Figure 1. Sugar cube pattern

Cube fold

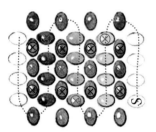

Cube side 1

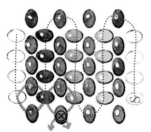

End of side 1

squares are separated by 4 white opal hinge rows. Begin at the S at the bottom left; finish at the bottom right white crossing bead along the right edge. This crossing bead is the starting point for zipping together the cube layers.

CUBE FOLD

STEP 2: Begin to zip up the edges of the squares. Fold the mat accordion-style into the "W" position indicated in the diagram, with the final unit's crossing bead in the "S" (South, starting) position. Check that the color sequence and white opal hinge beads at the folds match the diagram.

CUBE SIDE 1

Row 1, Unit 1, 90° turn to the East: Turn your folded cube so that the "S" bead is in the South position. String an opal West, pass through a Color 2 North, and string and cross through an opal East. Rotate your work 90° back to the original folded "W" position.

Row 1, Units 2 and 3, zip-up units: Pass through white East and Color 2 West, string opal North crossing bead.

Row 1, Unit 4, 90° turn to the West: Pass through white East, opal North, and Color 2 West crossing bead. Rotate your work 90° so the crossing bead is now in the South position.

Row 2, Unit 1, 90° turn to the West: String opal East, pass through Color 3 North, string opal West crossing bead. Rotate your work 90° so the crossing bead is now in the South position.

Row 2, Units 2 and 3, zip-up units: Pass through Color 2 West, Color 3 East, string opal North crossing bead.

Row 2, Unit 4, 90° turn to the East: Pass through Color 2 West, opal North, and Color 3 East crossing bead. Rotate your work 90° so the crossing bead is now in the South position.

Row 3, Unit 1, 90° turn to the East: String opal West, pass through Color 4 North, string opal East crossing bead. Rotate your work 90° so the crossing bead is now in the South position.

Row 3, Units 2 and 3, zip-up units: Pass through Color 3 East, Color 4 West, string opal North crossing bead.

Row 3, Unit 4, 90° turn to the West: Pass through Color 3 East, opal North, and Color 4 West crossing bead. Rotate your work 90° so the crossing bead is now in the South position.

Row 4, Unit 1, 90° turn to the West: String opal East, pass through white North, string opal West crossing bead. Rotate your work 90° so the crossing bead is now in the South position.

Row 4, Units 2 and 3, zip-up units: Pass through white East, Color 4 West, string opal North crossing bead.

Finish Side 1 with two turns, to get into position to work Side 2.

Turn Unit 1, 90° turn to the West: Pass through white East, opal North, Color 4 West crossing bead.

Turn Unit 2, 90° turn to the East: Pass through opal West, Color 3 North, opal East crossing bead. Rotate your work 90° so the crossing bead is now in the South position, and turn your cube to match the diagram for Side 2.

CUBE SIDE 2

STEP 3:   Zip together the edges of side 2.

Units 1 and 2, zip-up units: Pass through Color 4 East, Color 3 West, string opal North crossing bead.

Unit 3, 90° turn to the West: Pass through Color 4 East, string opal North, pass through Color 3 West crossing bead. Rotate your work 90° so the crossing bead is now in the South position.

Unit 4: Pass through opal East, opal West, and Color 2 North crossing bead.

Unit 5, 90° turn to the West: String opal East, pass through white North, string opal West crossing bead. Rotate your work 90° so the crossing bead is now in the South position.

Units 6 and 7, zip-up units: Pass through white East, Color 2 West, string opal North crossing bead.

Unit 8, 90° turn to the West: Pass through white East, opal North, Color 2 West. Tie a knot and conceal it inside the South bead.

CUBE SIDE 3

STEP 4:   Zip together the edges of side 3.

Start a new length of 18" of thread at the South "starting" bead indicated in the diagram. Work Rows 1–4 in the same manner as for side 1, the only difference being opal pass-throughs at two of the turns instead of new opal beads being strung. The two final end turns of side 1 are not required for side 3.

Row 4, final Unit 4: Pass through white East, Color 4 West, string opal North crossing bead. Turn your cube to match the diagram, with the crossing bead now in the South position.

CUBE SIDE 4

STEP 5:   Finish the edges of side 4.

Work the zip-ups and turns as for side 2, passing through the white opal beads at the turns instead of stringing new ones. This side zips up pairs of Color 5 (edged with white) and Color 4, and pairs of Colors 3 and 2. Tie the final knot in the same manner as for side 2. Trim the ends of both knots, and you're ready to start another cube!

Cube side 2

Cube side 3

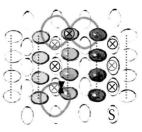

Cube side 4

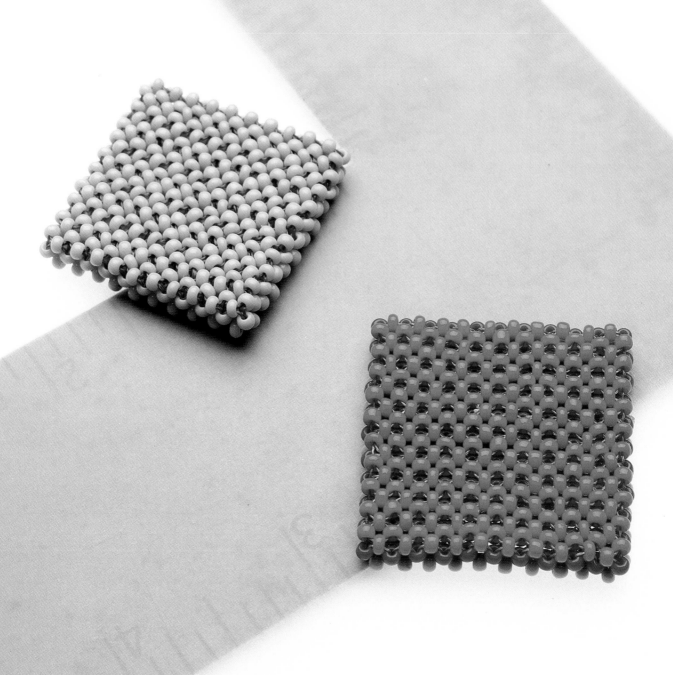

Chapter Nine

Frames, Tablets, and Triangles

Frames and tablet motifs open

the door to all sorts of design fun.

A frame can be reinforced by stringing

smaller beads between the beads forming

its edges, so you can make the piece as

flexible or rigid as you please. Now

think of all the beautiful beads and

charms you'd like to "frame!"

Frames

You can choose any of three ways to make a frame. In the very intuitive Method 1, two flat frames are constructed, and then the frames are zipped together along their outside and inside edges. While Method 2 may appear more complex, I actually find it easier to work and for noodling around in tight places—for example, attaching a frame to another piece of beadwork, as in our box project (on page 92) The third method is a variant of Method 2 for single-needle use, to avoid filling the bead holes with too much thread.

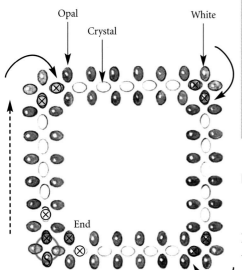

Figure 1. Frames base pattern

Opal
Crystal
White
End

MATERIALS
▨ *Size 10° seed beads in opaque green, crystal, white, and opal white*

Two-needle method:

▨ *2 yd of PowerPro thread*

Single-needle method:

▨ *3 yd of your preferred beading thread*

METHOD 1

STEP 1: Using 1 yd of thread, follow Figure 1 to make a square frame that is 8 units long on each side. The 4 beads forming each corner of the square are white; the sides are opal white for the East/West edges and crystal for the North/South beads.

STEP 2: Start a new length of 1 yd of thread, and make another square frame identical to the first, *except for the final unit make a 90° turn to the West, on the outside perimeter.* Rotate your work so that the crossing bead is in the South position for the next unit.

STEP 3: Stack your second frame atop the first, and zip them together with your thread from Step 2 by working a row along the outside perimeter, using green for the North crossing beads.

Unit 1, a 90° turn to the East to begin the zip-up row: String green West, pass through opal North on edge of lower frame, string green East crossing bead.

Units 2–31: Pass through opal East and West (or white East and West at the corners), string green North crossing bead.

Unit 32: Pass through white East, West, and green North.

If you wish to stiffen the frame, continue around the outside frame edges adding smaller (size 11° or 15°) reinforcing beads between the edge beads. Otherwise, tie a concealed knot and trim the thread.

STEP 4: Using your thread from Step 1, zip up the inside edge of the frame.

Unit 1, a 90° turn to the East to begin the zip-up row: String green West, pass through opal North on edge of other frame, string green East crossing bead.

Units 2–22: Pass through opal East and West, string green North crossing bead.

Unit 23: Pass through opal East, green North, opal West.

If you wish to stiffen the frame, continue around the inside frame edges adding smaller (size 11° or 15°) reinforcing beads between the edge beads. Otherwise, tie a concealed knot and trim the thread.

METHOD 2

STEP 1: Follow Figure 1 to make a square frame that is 8 units long on each side. The 4 beads forming each corner of the square are white; the sides are opal white for the East/West edges and crystal for the North/South beads.

Inside flange start

STEP 2: Work a row around the inside edge of the frame base to form a flange that stands up at a right angle to the base (Figure 2).

Unit 1, a 90° turn to the East: String green West, opal North, and green East crossing bead. Rotate your work so that the crossing bead is in the South position for the next unit.

Units 2–22: Pass through opal East, string opal West, green North crossing bead. The corners will form automatically as you work around the inside edge of the frame.

Inside flange end

Unit 23, a 90° turn to the West: Pass through opal East and green North, string opal East crossing bead. Rotate your work so that the crossing bead is in the South position for the next unit (Figure 3).

Crossover to beginning of outside flange

STEP 3: Work 2 units to cross over to the

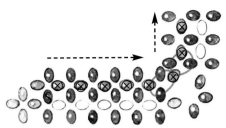

Figure 2. Inside flange start

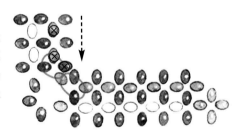

Figure 3. Inside flange end

Figure 4. Crossover to outside flange start

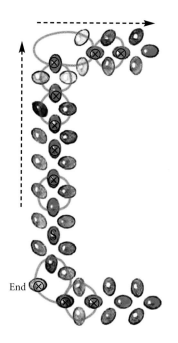

End

Figure 5. Outside flange

outside edge of the frame base to start an outside flange that stands up at a right angle to the base (Figure 4).

Unit 1: String white West, crystal East, opal North crossing bead.

Unit 2, a 90° turn to the East: String green West, pass through opal North on outside edge of frame base, string green East crossing bead. Rotate your work so that the crossing bead is in the South position for the next unit.

Outside flange

STEP 4: Work a row around the outside edge of the frame base to form a flange that stands up at a right angle to the base (Figure 5). Be careful at the start of this flange to get your orientation right—imagine the flange as being turned outward from the base, like the left-hand cover of a book. Your South starting bead will be rotated outward (loosen up the previous unit, if necessary, to see this effect). If you're using two needles, it will seem as if the East and West threads switch positions. If you're using one needle, the thread will now seem to emerge from the opposite hole of the bead, and the direction of the next unit will seem to be the same as the previous unit. In other words, if Unit 2 of the crossover was a clockwise unit, you might expect the next unit to be counter-clockwise; but no, the starting bead is rotated outward 180°, and so the next unit will also be clockwise.

Units 1–5: Pass through opal East on frame base, string opal West and green North crossing bead.

Unit 6 and 7, at corner: Pass through white East on frame base, string white West and green North crossing bead.

Units 8–30: Continue to work the sides of the flange as in Unit 1, and the corners as in Units 6 and 6.

Unit 31, a 90° turn to the West: Pass through white East and green North, string white West crossing bead. Rotate your work so that the crossing bead is in the South position for the next unit.

Zipping together inside and outside flanges

STEP 5: Zip together the inside and outside flanges (Figure 6).

Unit 1: Pass through white West (part of Unit 2 from the Step 3 crossover), pass through white East on outside flange edge, string white North crossing bead.

Units 2–6: Pass through flange edge beads opal East and opal West, string crystal North crossing bead.

Unit 7: Pass through opal East and West, string white North crossing bead.

Unit 8, a 90° turn to the West: Pass through white East and white North on outside corner, string white West crossing bead.

Rotate your work so that the crossing bead is in the South position for the next unit.

Continue around the frame. Units 9–13, 16–21, and 23–27 are the same as Unit 2 (opal East and West, crystal North crossing bead).

Units 14 and 21 are the same as Unit 7.

Corner Units 15 and 22 are the same as Unit 8.

If you wish to stiffen the frame, continue around the frames edges adding smaller (size 11° or 15°) reinforcing beads between the inside and outside edge beads. Otherwise, tie a concealed knot inside the North bead in Unit 27 and trim thread ends.

METHOD 3 ALTERNATE SINGLE-NEEDLE METHOD

When using a single needle, working the steps as in Methods 1 or 2 may fill up the bead holes with too much thread. If you plan to further embellish your frame, this could create difficulties. Create a frame using Method 2 above in order to learn the pattern, then try another frame using the method below, and see which you prefer.

STEP 1 and STEP 2: Construct the frame and inside flange as in Method 2.

STEP 3: A 90° turn to the East, combining Units 1 and 2 from Method 2, Step 3 above. String white West, opal North with a picot downward (string opaque, pass back through opal on outside edge of frame base, string green, pass again through opal North), string green East crossing bead.

Rotate your work so that the crossing bead is in the South position for the next unit.

STEP 4: Build the outside flange and top connection row simultaneously with similar "bent-wing" or "sideways" figure-eight units as described for Step 3, *with a picot dropping down from each West bead to connect the top to the frame base, creating the outside flange as you go.* The crossing bead is North. Note that at the corners the North bead from the prior unit becomes the West bead for the next unit, and so two picots are needed at the corner units.

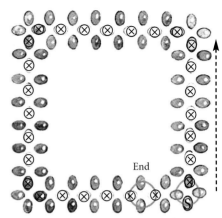

Figure 6. Zip-up inside and outside flanges

Tablets

These three-layer bead sandwiches are rigid enough to stand alone as pendants, serve as backs for cabochon brooches, or to form the tops and bottoms of boxes. If the two outer layers are transparent and the interior layer is opaque, subtle color blends can be achieved. For instance, in a tablet with light yellow transparent outer layers, an opaque inner layer of red or orange will create a "holographic" effect of golden orange. Or, an inner layer of green and/or blue will change the yellow to chartreuse or lime.

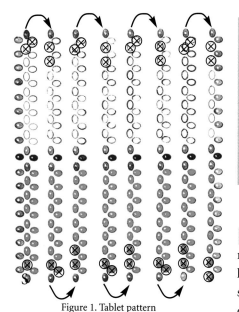

Figure 1. Tablet pattern

STEP 1: Starting at the bottom left corner, follow Figure 1 to make a mat 17 units long by 8 rows wide. Two transparent 8 × 8 squares (one rose, one crystal, edged with opaque white) are separated by an opal white hinge. Finish the mat at the bottom right white crossing bead and tie a temporary knot to hold the beads together, leaving the threads to finish off later.

STEP 2: Start a new length of thread at the opal bead at one end of the opal hinge row and rotate your work so that this is the South crossing bead. You'll be "gluing" the two squares together with a series of edge units of white and opal and interior zip-up rows of blue.

Row 1, Edge Unit 1: Pass through white East and West, string opal North crossing bead (Figure 2).

INTERIOR ZIP-UP ROW OF TABLET

Row 1, Interior Units 2–8: Pass through East and West transparent colors, string blue North crossing bead (Figure 3).

Row 1, Unit 9: Pass through East and West transparent colors, string opal North crossing bead.

EDGE UNIT ALONG SIDE OF TABLET

Row 1, Unit 10, an edge unit along the tablet side: If you're using two needles, just use one for this unit. It's a "picot," with no new beads being strung. Pass through white, opal, white, then pass again through the opal crossing bead from Unit 7 (Figure 4). You'll discover that it's convenient to keep going through either the next white East or West edge bead to get a jump start on the next row.

Rows 2–7 are the same as Row 1.

Row 8, Edge Units 1–9, forming the final nar-row side of the tablet: Pass through white East and West, string opal North crossing bead.

Row 8, Edge Unit 10, a picot.

Tie knots and conceal them inside beads, then trim thread ends.

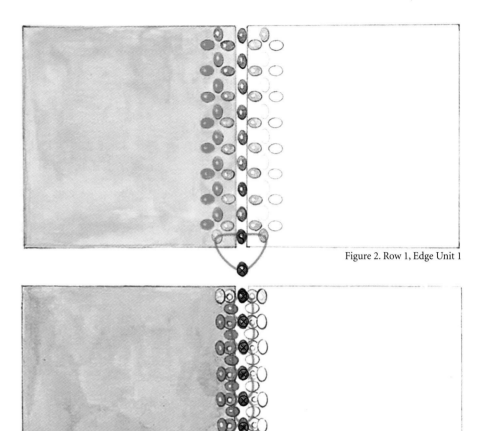

Figure 2. Row 1, Edge Unit 1

Figure 3. Row 1, Interior Units 2–8

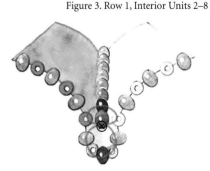

Figure 4. Edge Unit, tablet side

Triangle Tablets

I love the way these can be used as beaded findings, especially as strand separators as in the sample necklace—not to mention the fun color-change effects from the hidden inside layer, and the way the edge beads conveniently position themselves as anchor points for further embellishment.

MATERIALS

▨ *Size 10° seed beads in white opal, crystal, transparent aqua, white, and opaque blue*

Two needles:

▨ *2' of PowerPro for the first half-diamond, 1 yd for the second, 10lb test*

Single needle:

▨ *1 yd of your preferred thread for the first half-diamond, 1½ yd for the second*

Making diamonds and triangles is an excellent way to learn to love figure-eight increases and decreases. However, this does also make them one of the most difficult projects in this book! I recommend making a square tablet first in order to understand the process before tackling a triangle tablet. Once you've made your triangle, however, you'll have earned your right-angle Weave Commando badge!

WORK IDENTICAL HALF-DIAMONDS, JOIN THEM WITH A CENTER HINGE

For our little triangle tablet separator, make two right-triangle pieces, join them with a hinge row along their long sides, and then "glue" them together with edge units and interior zip-up rows. I find figure-eight increases easier than figure-eight decreases (which require planning ahead—always more difficult!), so our sample features two 4-row right triangles that build from the 90° angle toward the long edge. Figure 6, page 91 shows 9 rows if you wish to make larger triangle tablets. It also shows how to make the two triangles in one piece, in a manner similar to the square tablet pattern—if you don't mind making decreases as well as increases. See page 37 in the Turns chapter for detailed figure-eight instructions.

STEP 1: Refer to Figure 1 to make a 4-row triangle, beginning at the left 90°-angle point.

Row 1, Unit 1: String opal South and West, crystal East and North crossing bead.

Row 1, Unit 2, a 90° turn to the East: String opal West and North, crystal East crossing bead. Rotate your work so that the crossing bead is in the South position for the next unit.

Row 2, Units 1 and 2, a figure-eight turn to the East: Refer to page 37 for this type of turn. String new beads in these positions: crystal West, crystal 8N, opal 8W, opal 8S, crystal North, crystal East crossing bead. Rotate your work so that the crossing bead is in the South position for the next unit.

Row 2, Unit 3: Pass through crystal East, string crystal West and crystal North crossing bead.

Row 2, Unit 4, a 90° turn to the West: String opal East and North, crystal West crossing bead. Rotate your work so that the crossing bead is in the South position for the next unit.

Row 3, Units 1 and 2, a figure-eight increase and turn to the West: Refer to page 38 for this type of turn. String new beads in these positions: crystal East, crystal 8N, opal 8E, opal 8S, crystal North, crystal West crossing bead.

Rotate your work so that the crossing bead is in the South position for the next unit.

Row 3, Units 3–5: Pass through crystal East from previous row, string crystal West and crystal North crossing bead.

Row 3, Unit 6, a 90° turn to the East: String opal West and North, crystal East crossing bead.

Rotate your work so that the crossing bead is in the South position for the next unit.

Row 4, Units 1 and 2, a figure-eight increase and turn to the East: String new beads in these positions: crystal West, crystal 8N, opal 8W, opal 8S, crystal North, crystal East crossing bead.

Row 4, Units 3–7: Pass through crystal East, string opal West and crystal North crossing bead.

Row 4, Unit 8, a 90° turn to the West: String opal East, North, and West crossing bead.

Tie a temporary knot, if necessary, and leave thread end(s) to be finished later.

STEP 2: Start a new length of thread for the second triangle, and work it similarly to the first, only using transparent aqua instead of crystal. Do not tie a knot at the end of the last row.

STEP 3: Arrange the triangles as in Figure

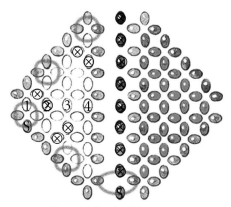

Figure 1. Triangle tablets pattern

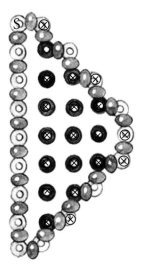

Figure 2

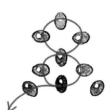

Figure 3

Figure 4

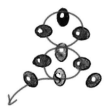

Figure 5

1. Using the thread(s) exiting the last crossing bead of the second triangle, connect the two triangles with a hinge row.

Hinge Row, Unit 1, a 90° turn to the East: String white East, pass through the first opal on the long edge of the first triangle, and string white West crossing bead. Rotate your work so that the crossing bead is in the South position for the next unit.

Hinge Row 1, Units 2–8: Pass through opal East and West on adjacent sides and string white North crossing bead.

STEP 4: Fold the two triangles along the hinge and then "glue" them together with a series of edge units in white and opal, and interior zip-up rows in blue (Figure 2).

Row 1, Edge Unit 1: Pass through opal East and West on adjacent sides and string white North crossing bead.

Row 1, Unit 2: Pass through opal East and West, string blue North crossing bead.

Row 1, Units 3–8: Pass through crystal and aqua East and West, string blue North crossing bead.

First figure-eight pass through at the end of interior zip-up Row 1

Row 1, Figure-eight Edge Unit 9: Referring to Figure 3, make a figure-eight. Pass through opal, string white, pass through opal, white, opal, and again through "new" white, pass through opal and again through blue crossing bead from Unit 8. You'll discover that it's convenient to keep going through either the next white East or West edge bead to get a jump start on the next row. Rotate your work so that the crossing bead is in the South position for the next unit.

Row 2, Units 1–6: Same as Row 1.

Subsequent figure-eight pass throughs at the ends of interior zip-up rows

Row 2, Figure-eight Edge Unit 7: (Figure 4) Pass through opal, string white, pass through opal, blue, opal, pass again through "new" white, pass through opal, pass through blue crossing bead from prior unit, and continue on through the first opal bead of the next edge unit.

Row 3, Units 1–5: Same as Row 2

Row 4, Edge Unit 1: Same as Row 1

Row 4, Triangle Point Unit 2: Pass through opal East and West on adjacent sides and string white North crossing bead (Figure 5).

Row 4, Figure-eight Edge Unit 3: Pass through opal, string white, pass through opal, blue, opal, pass again through "new" white, pass through opal, pass through white crossing bead from Unit 2.

Tie concealed knots and trim the thread ends.

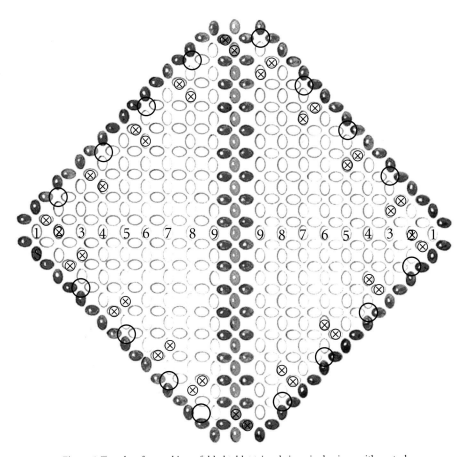

1 2 3 4 5 6 7 8 9 9 8 7 6 5 4 3 2 1

Figure 6. Template for working a folded tablet triangle in a single piece, with central hinge and figure-eight increases and decreases

BONUS CHALLENGE

Following the pattern in Figure 7, make stripes on the sides of your triangles as in the lariat project.

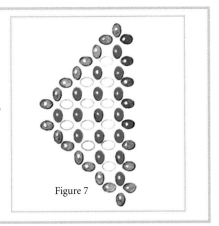

Figure 7

Lidded Box

Construct a sturdy little box using a combination
of tablet and frame techniques.

MATERIALS

Czech size 10° seed beads in red, coral, and turquoise

Czech size 12° seed beads in red

Faux coral polymer clay cabochon, 25 × 21mm

PowerPro 10lb test, moss color

LID

STEP 1: Make a tablet that is 4 units longer than the length and width of the cabochon. Our sample measures 13 × 11 units. Coral beads were used for the interior zip-up layer, with red along the edges.

STEP 2: Surround the cabochon with a rectangular bezel similar to the inside flange of a frame. Center the cabochon on your tablet, and then start the bezel in the middle of the shorter 11-unit row along the short edge of the cabochon, 3 East/West beads in from the tablet edge. Work around

Inside of box lid

the cabochon twice, making the bezel flange 2 rows high. String size 12° reinforcing beads between the beads forming the upper edge of the bezel, skipping the corners. Pull the thread(s) to cinch the bezel tightly against the cabochon. Tie a concealed knot, work the thread(s) downward to bury the end(s) a ways, then trim.

STEP 3: Using the turquoise beads, make a frame on the bottom of the lid to form a lip to keep the lid from sliding off the box. Start with the inside flange, centering each of its sides 4 East/West beads in from the tablet edges. This will allow a bare tablet row all around to sit atop the sides of the box.

STEP 4: String size 10° reinforcing beads (coral) between the beads along the outer top and bottom edges of the lid. Tie a concealed knot and trim the thread.

BOX

STEP 1: Make a tablet for the bottom of the box identical in size to the lid. Our sample box has a diamond pattern worked into the two outer layers (Figure 1; the interior zip-up layer is coral, with red at the edges).

STEP 2: Make a frame atop the bottom tablet, starting the inside flange (the lining of the box) 2 beads in from the edge (in our sample, the inner flange/lining is coral). Coral beads are also used for the row that zips together the inside and outside flanges of the frame. Working upward, construct three more frames atop the first, for a total of four frames.

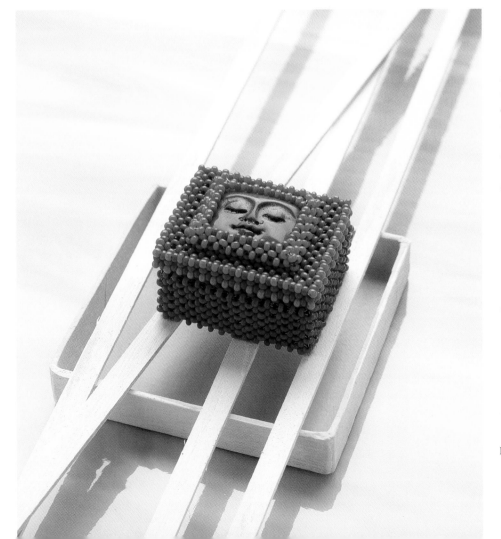

Figure 1. Box base tablet outside and inside pattern

Right-Angle Lariat

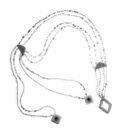

This beautfiul necklace incorporates just about everything you've
learned to do with right-angle weave: tablets, frames, and triangles.

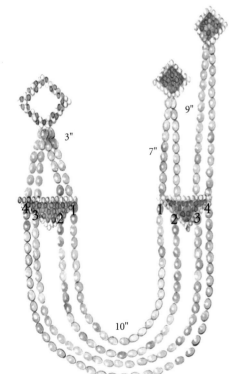

Figure 1. Right-angle lariat pattern

MATERIALS

▨ *8 × 8 unit frame*

▨ *Two 5 × 5 unit tablets (same pattern as for cube faces in the "Bead in a Box" project, using transparent crystal and green beads for the interior zip-up layer)*

▨ *Two 4-row triangle tablets (striped as in the "Bonus Challenge" pattern at the end
of the "Triangle Tablet" section)*

▨ *360–400 Czech glass "pinch" beads (5 × 3mm three-sided ovals)—crystal and
peridot in sample*

▨ *Size 10° or 11° crystal luster seed beads*

▨ *8 size 15° crystal rainbow seed beads*

▨ *4 yd PowerPro 10lb test, cut into two lengths*

▨ *Size 10 beading needle*

STEP 1: See Figure 1. Pass one length of
thread through the inside corner bead of the
frame, centering it and running each end out
on either side of the bead forming the outside corner edge. String 15 pinch beads on
each end. Pass one end through the base of

a triangle tablet in the "2" position, and the
other end through the "3" position.

STEP 2: Pass the other length of thread
through the inside corner bead of the frame,
but this time run each end out at a 90° angle

94

to the first, again on either side of the outside corner edge bead. Center the thread and string about 3" of beads (or 15 pinch beads) on each end, and then pass the threads through a triangle tablet in the "1" and "4" positions.

STEP 3: String at least 10–11" of beads (60 pinch beads in the sample) for the inside strand and pass through the "1" position of the second triangle spacer. Arrange your work as in the diagram so that this strand forms a U-shaped loop. String the remaining strands with sufficient beads so that they drape at least ¼" from the first strand and from one another.

STEP 4: For the two long lariat ends emerging from positions 3 and 4 of the sec-

ond triangle, string about 9" of beads (in the sample, 20 pinch beads followed by 21 pinch beads separated by a size 10° seed bead). For the two short lariat ends, string about 7" of beads (20 pinch beads followed by 15 beads separated by size 10° seed beads).

STEP 5: Attach each pair of strands to a tablet via the center edge beads on either side of a corner point by stringing a size 15° seed bead, passing through the edge bead, and stringing another 15° bead. Draw up the beads on the strand so that they're sufficiently tight without unsightly gaps, and tie an overhand knot around the thread between the size 15° beads and the last pinch bead on each strand. Pass back through the beads on the strand, tying multi-overhand knots after each of the first 4 seed beads.

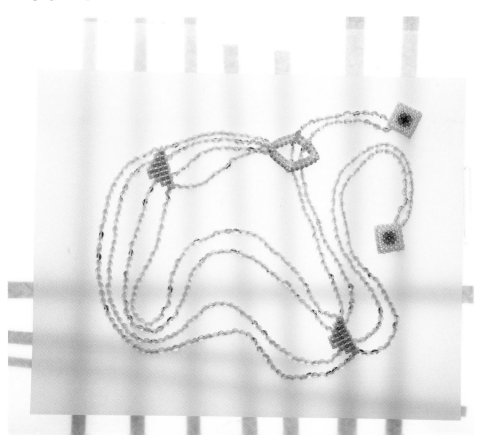

Gallery

Here you'll find a sampling of

amazing right-angle weave designs

from beadists around the country. Some

projects took years to create; some took

only a few hours . . . yet they're all, in

their own ways, stunning works of art

and whimsy.

Nancy Zellers, Denver, Colorado.
Orange, the Other Neutral
Seed beads over wooden base. 11" H × 8" W × 8" D.

Nancy Zellers, Denver, Colorado.
Queen of the Night
Seed beads over wooden base. 22" L × 16" W × 14" H.

Nancy Zellers, Denver, Colorado.
Golden Gumdrops Necklaces
Seed beads over ⅞" resin beads. 12" L.

Ella Johnson-Bentley, Juneau, Alaska.
Let's Play
Seed beads, lampwork beads, ribbon.
Bag 5½" L × 4¾" W; jacks 1½ × 1¾"; ball 1⅜" D.

Ella Johnson-Bentley, Juneau, Alaska.
Fruit Bowl
Seed beads over forms. Bowl 3½" H × 4¾" D; doily 6½" D.

Ella Johnson-Bentley, Juneau, Alaska.
One, Two, Buckle My Shoe
Seed beads, fabric, three-dimensional right-angle weave. LaCrosse boot, 4" L × 2¾" H;
clown shoe, 4¼" L × 2¼" H; brown shoe with buckle, 4" L × 1¼" H.

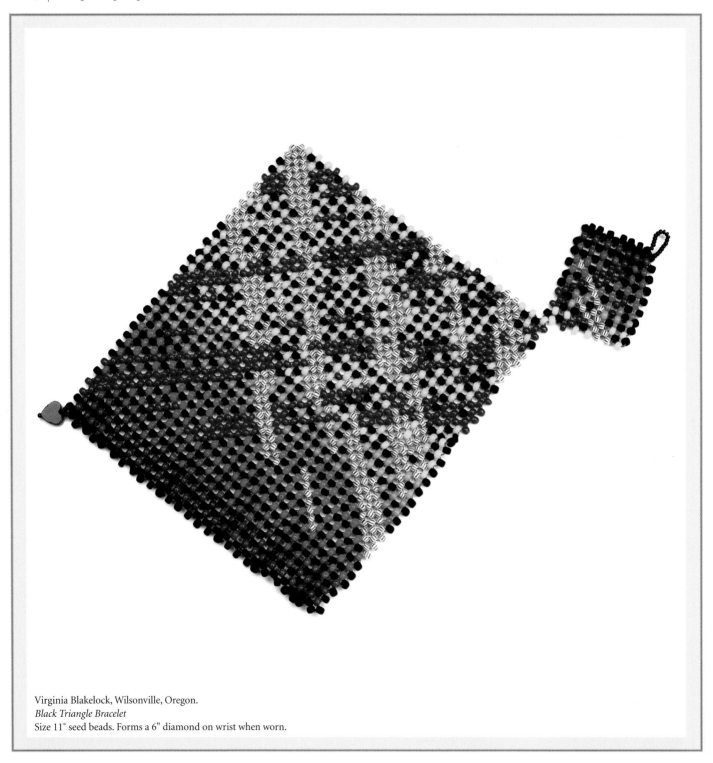

Virginia Blakelock, Wilsonville, Oregon.
Black Triangle Bracelet
Size 11° seed beads. Forms a 6" diamond on wrist when worn.

Ella Johnson-Bentley, Juneau, Alaska.
Sock It To Me
Seed beads stuffed with batting. 12" H with tail.

Janet Francis, Ellington, Connecticut.
Crystal Plaid Necklace
Seed beads and Swarovski crystals. 9" L.

Janet Francis, Ellington, Connecticut.
Servo Bag
Seed beads, bugle beads, crystals, plastic housing for a servo-motor for the cruise control for a 1988 Chrysler LeBaron.
7¼" H (base 1¾" H) × 4½" D.

Janet Francis, Ellington, Connecticut.
Garnet Embers Necklace
Seed beads, Swarovski crystals, jet tear drop beads. 8" L w/fringe.

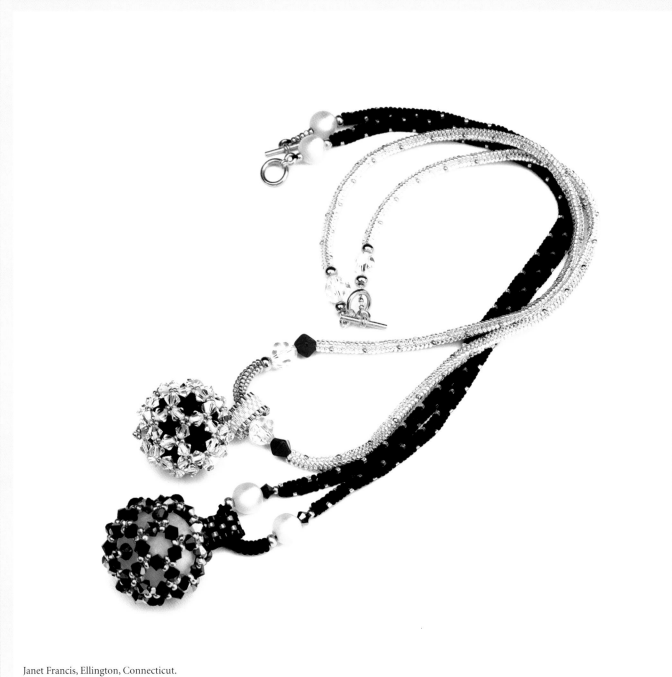

Janet Francis, Ellington, Connecticut.
Solomon's Seal Talisman Bead Necklaces
Seed beads, Delicas, Swarovski crystals, clasps.
White, 11½" L, ball 1" D; Black, 11" L, ball 1" D.

Ella Johnson-Bentley, Juneau, Alaska
Chili Peppers Necklace
Seed beads, bugle beads, pressed glass. 18" L.

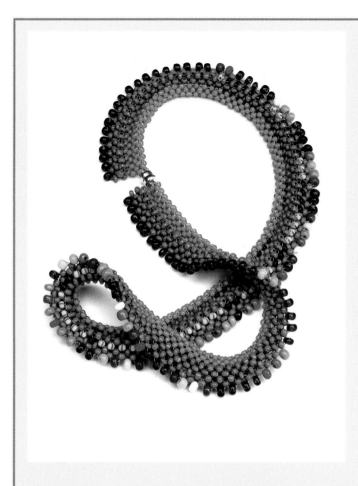

Christine Prussing, Juneau, Alaska
Graduated Seed Bead Collar
Seed beads. 8½" L.

Mel Jonassen, Norwich, Connecticut.
120 Flavors
Seed bead woven curtain and covered dowel. 30" W × 14" L.

Dustin Wedekind, Fort Collins, Colorado.
Right Amber Wave
Fossilized cabochon, amber nuggets, freshwater pearls,
Czech fire-polished and seed beads. 9" L.

Ella Johnson-Bentley, Juneau, Alaska.
Fantasy Fruit
Seed beads worked over plastic forms. Apples, pears, peach 4½" circumference,
orange 4¼" circumference, smaller pieces 2¾" circumference.

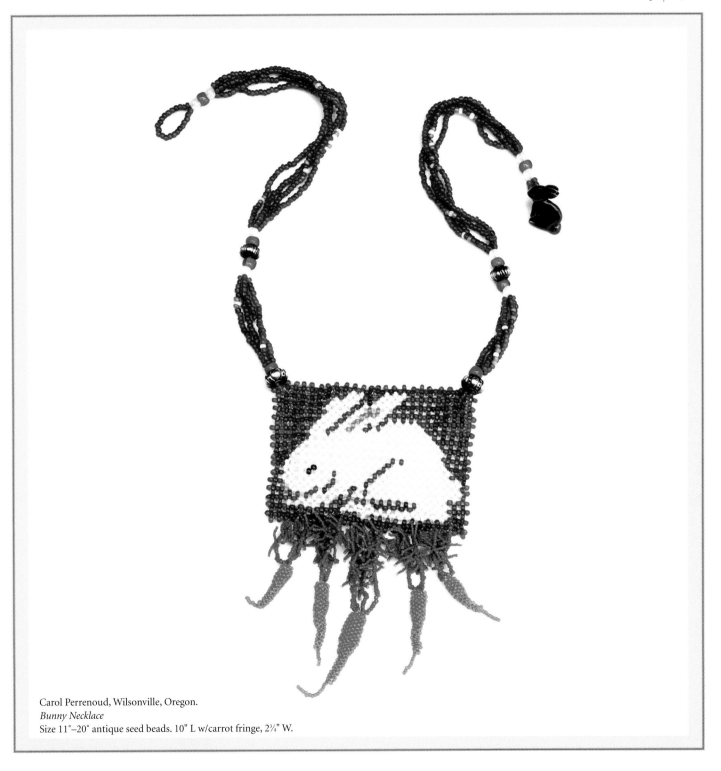

Carol Perrenoud, Wilsonville, Oregon.
Bunny Necklace
Size 11°–20° antique seed beads. 10" L w/carrot fringe, 2¾" W.

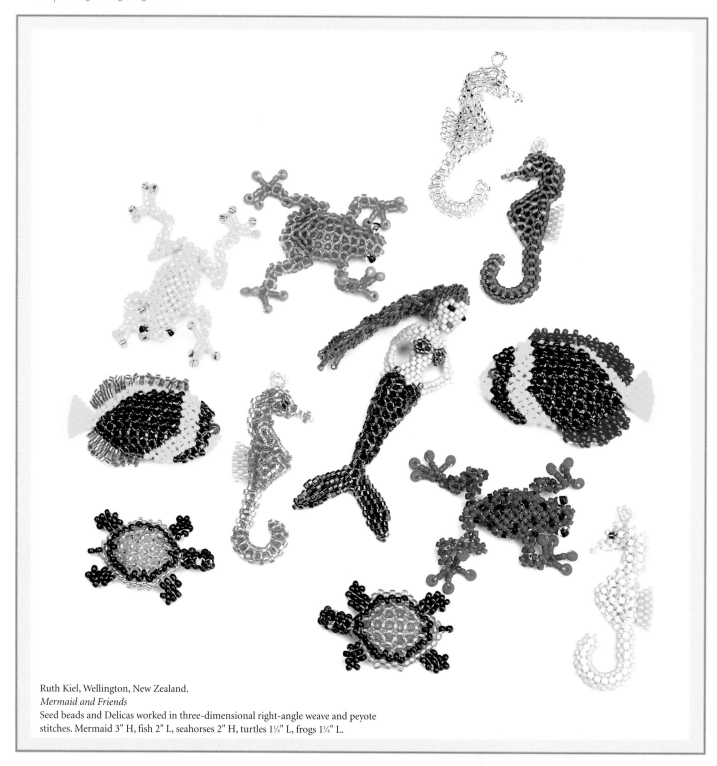

Ruth Kiel, Wellington, New Zealand.
Mermaid and Friends
Seed beads and Delicas worked in three-dimensional right-angle weave and peyote
stitches. Mermaid 3" H, fish 2" L, seahorses 2" H, turtles 1¼" L, frogs 1¼" L.

Christine Prussing, Juneau, Alaska.
Diagonally Striped Crystal Ribbon Necklace
Fire-polished Czech glass, seed beads, pearls. 14¼" L.

Christine Prussing, Juneau, Alaska.
Jade and Turquoise Necklace
Jade and turquoise beads. 14½" L.

Bibliography

Anufrieva, M.Y. *Art of Bead-Weaving.* Moscow: Kultura I Tradicii, 2002.

Bateman. Sharon. *Findings & Finishings.* Loveland, Colorado: Interweave Press, 2003.

Blakelock, Virginia L. *Those Bad, Bad Beads.* Wilsonville, Oregon: Virginia L. Blakelock, 1990.

Campbell, Jean, editor. *Beadwork Creates Bracelets.* Loveland, Colorado: Interweave Press, 2002.
_____. *Beadwork Creates Beaded Bags.* Loveland, Colorado: Interweave Press, 2002.
_____. *Beadwork Creates Beaded Beads.* Loveland, Colorado: Interweave Press, 2002.
_____. *Beadwork Creates Necklaces.* Loveland, Colorado: Interweave Press, 2002.

Cassidy, John. *The Klutz Book of Knots: How to Tie the World's 24 Most Useful Hitches, Ties, Wraps, and Knots.* Palo Alto, California: Klutz, 1985.

Clarke, Amy C., and Robin Atkins. *Beaded Embellishment: Techniques and Designs for Embroidering on Cloth.* Loveland, Colorado: Interweave Press, 2002.

Cook, Jeannette, and Vicki Star. *Beady Eyed Women's Guide to Exquisite Beadwork: An Off-Loom Bead Weaving Primer.* San Diego, California: Beady Eyed Women Enterprises, 1996.

Crabtree, Caroline, and Pam Stallebrass. *Beadwork: A World Guide.* New York: Rizzoli, 2002.

Glass Bead Artistry. Tokyo: Ondorisha Publishers, Ltd., 1992.

Glassman, Judith. *Step-By-Step Beadcraft.* New York: Golden Press, 1974.

Goodhue, Horace. *Indian Beadweaving Patterns.* St. Paul, Minnesota: Bead-Craft, 1984.

Hector, Valerie. "Prosperity, Reverence and Protection: An Introduction to Asian Beadwork." *Beads: Journal of the Society of Bead Researchers,* Volume 7 (1995), 3–36.

LaCroix, Grethe. *Creating With Beads.* New York: Sterling Publishing Co., Inc., 1969.

Meng, Ho Wing. *Straits Chinese Beadwork and Embroidery: A Collector's Guide.* Singapore: Times Books International, 1987.

Moiseenko, Elena, and Valeria Faleeva. *Beadwork and Bugle in Russia: 18th—Early 20th Century*. Leningrad: Khudoznik RSFSR, 1990.

Moss, Kathlyn, and Alice Scherer. *The New Beadwork*. New York: Harry N. Abrams, Inc., 1992.

Muto, Mitsuko. *Basic Beadwork for Beginners*. Tokyo: Ondorisha Publishers, Ltd., 1996.

Nathanson, Virginia. *The Pearl and Bead Boutique Book*. Great Neck, New York: The Hearthside Press, Inc., 1972.

Orchard, William C. *Beads and Beadwork of the American Indians: A Study Based on Specimens in the Museum of the American Indian, Heye Foundation*. Liberty, Utah: Eagle's View Publishing, 2000.

Rodgers, Carole. *Right-Angle Weave Beading 101*. Fort Worth, Texas: Design Originals by Suzanne McNeill, 2002.

Root, Gineke. *Innovative Beaded Jewelry Techniques*. Berkeley, California: Lacis Publications, 1994.

Rypan, Maria. *Gerdany: Beadwork Ukrainian-Style*. Toronto: Rypan Designs, 1996.
_____. *Gerdany: Beadwork Ukrainian-Style: Assorted Beadwork, Lessons #1*. Toronto: Rypan Designs, 2002.

Samejima, Takako. *Bead Fantasies: Beautiful, Easy-to-Make Jewelry*. Tokyo: Japan Publications Trading Co., 2003.

Seiler-Baldinger, Annemarie. *Textiles: A Classification of Techniques*. Washington, D.C.: Smithsonian Institution Press, 1994.

Stessin, Nicolette. *Beaded Amulet Purses*. Seattle, Washington: Beadworld Publishing, 1994.

Wells, Carol Wilcox. *Creative Beadweaving*. Asheville, North Carolina: Lark Books, 1996.

White, Mary. *How to Do Beadwork*. New York: Doubleday, Page & Co., 1904.

Walco Bead Co. *Wood Bead Craft: Instructions and Designs for the Making of Bags, Necklaces, Bracelets, Belts (Walco Bead-Crafts Booklet No. 21)*. New York: Walco Bead Co., 1937.

Resources

Beadcats/Universal Synergetics
PO Box 2840
Wilsonville, OR 97070
(503) 625-2323
(503) 625-4329 fax
www.beadcats.com

Bead-Patterns.com
Sova Enterprises
948 Eubank Blvd. N.E.
Albuquerque, NM 87112-5308
(505) 262-2548
(505) 262-1364 fax
www.bead-patterns.com

Beyond Beadery
PO Box 460-BB
Rollinsville, CO 80474-0460
(800) 840-5548
(866) FAX-BEAD fax
www.beyondbeadery.com

Caravan Beads
449 Forest Ave.
Portland, ME 04101
(800) 230-8941
(207) 874-2664 fax
www.caravanbeads.com

Crazy Crow Trading Post & Bovis Bead Co.
PO Box 847 D-14
Pottsboro, TX 75076
(800) 786-6210
www.crazycrow.com

Innovative Textiles, Inc.
2105 I-70 B
Grand Junction, CO 81501
www.powerpro.com

Out On A Whim
121 E. Cotati Ave.
Cotati, CA 94931
(800) 232-3111
www.whimbeads.com

Rings & Things
PO Box 450
Spokane, WA 99270-0450
(800) 235-8517
(509) 838-2602 fax
www.rings-things.com

Rio Grande
(800) 545-6566
(800) 965-2329 fax
www.riogrande.com

Stormcloud Trading (Beadstorm)
725 Snelling Ave. N.
St. Paul, MN 55104
(651) 645-0343
www.beadstorm.com

ThatBeadLady.com
175 Crossland Gate
Newmarket, ON
Canada L3X 1A7
(905) 853-6179
(905) 853-6179 fax
www.thatbeadlady.com

Index